Aquatic Miniatures

A TIME-LIFE TELEVISION BOOK

Editor: Charles Osborne
Associate Editors: Bonnie Johnson, Joan Chambers
   Author: Don Earnest
   Writers: Cecilia Waters, Deborah Heineman
   Literary Research: Ellen Schachter
   Text Research: Maureen Duffy Benziger
Picture Editor: Judith Greene
   Permissions and Production: Cecilia Waters
Designer: Constance A. Timm
   Art Assistant: Patricia Byrne
Copy Editor: Eleanore W. Karsten
Copy Staff: Robert Braine, Florence Tarlow

WILD, WILD WORLD OF ANIMALS
TELEVISION PROGRAM
Producers: Jonathan Donald and Lothar Wolff
This Time-Life Television book is published by Time-Life Films, Inc.
Bruce L. Paisner, *President*
J. Nicoll Durrie, *Vice President*

THE AUTHOR

DON EARNEST was formerly a staff writer and editor with TIME-LIFE BOOKS. He has contributed to two previous volumes in this series, *Insects & Spiders* and *Birds of Field & Forest,* is co-author of *Life in the Coral Reef* and author of *Songbirds* and *Life in Zoos and Preserves.*

THE CONSÚLTANTS

JOHN COOKE is a director of Oxford Scientific Films Ltd. He is an invertebrate zoologist, a world authority on spiders and their relatives and a specialist in biological still photography. Before joining O. S. F. he lectured at Oxford University and was a member of the staff of The American Museum of Natural History in New York City.

ERNST KIRSTEUER is chairman and curator of the Department of Invertebrates at The American Museum of Natural History. He specializes in the study of marine worms and has published numerous articles on the subject in scientific journals.

THE COVER: A highly magnified larva of a mantis shrimp displays crustacean characteristics even at this immature stage. Its stalked compound eyes can see in almost all directions, although the antennae on top of its head are probably its most important sensory organs. Behind its eye stalks are the large claws that, as an adult, it will use to seize its prey.

Wild, Wild World of Animals

Aquatic
Miniatures

Based on the television series
Wild, Wild World of Animals

Published by
TIME-LIFE FILMS

The excerpt from The Center of Life by L. L. Larison Cudmore, copyright © 1977 by L. L. Larison Cudmore, is reprinted by permission of Times Books Div. of Quadrangle Books/The New York Times Book Co.

The excerpt from The Great Chain of Life by Joseph Wood Krutch, copyright © 1956 by Joseph Wood Krutch, is reprinted by permission of Houghton Mifflin Company.

The poem "The Microbe," from Cautionary Verses by Hilaire Belloc, published 1941 by Alfred A. Knopf, Inc., is reprinted by permission of Alfred A. Knopf, Inc., and Gerald Duckworth and Co., Ltd. (London).

The excerpt from Under the Sea Wind by Rachel L. Carson, copyright © 1941 by Rachel L. Carson, new ed. with corrections 1952, copyright renewed © 1968 by Roger Christie, is printed by permission of Oxford University Press, Inc., and Marie Rodell-Frances Collin Literary Agency.

The excerpt from Kon-Tiki by Thor Heyerdahl, copyright © 1950 by Thor Heyerdahl, is reprinted by permission of Rand McNally & Co. and George Allen & Unwin Ltd.

ISBN 0-913948-25-X.

Library of Congress catalogue card number: 78-73641.

Printed in the United States of America.

Contents

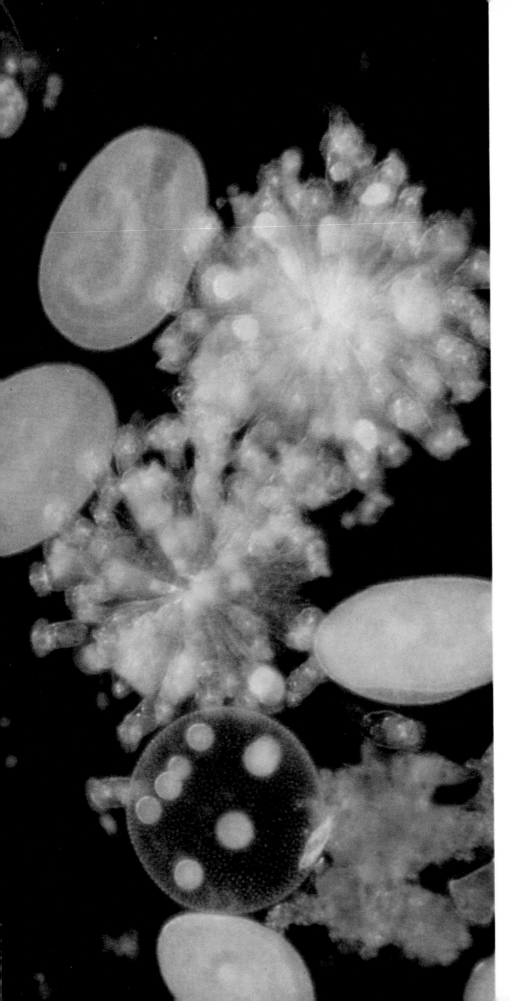

Introduction

by Don Earnest

To A PERSON UNINSTRUCTED IN NATURAL HISTORY," wrote the great 19th Century English zoologist T. H. Huxley, "his country or seaside stroll is a walk through a gallery filled with wonderful works of art, nine-tenths of which have their faces turned to the wall." It was a general observation, but the remark had special significance for Huxley himself about an area of particular interest to him: the smaller inhabitants of salt and fresh water. In the 1840s, Huxley was among the first to study the sea's smaller denizens, but there was then no way for him or other biologists to guess how vast was the trove of miniature masterpieces in the world's waters. These waters have turned out to be filled with galaxies of tiny beings so bizarre that even the most inventive science fantasist would be hard put to match them.

Observed under a microscope, a drop of seawater on a glass slide looks like the contents of a jewelry box spilled on a table. There are creatures that resemble oval, rectangular and triangular gems with intricate embossing, others that are shaped like miniature vases, anchors, necklaces, pendants, beads and mushrooms. Some are fringed, others have needle-like projections. A few even glimmer like stars. Most of these beings are minuscule one-celled plants and animals with glassy shells manufactured from minerals in the water. Sharing the waters with these creatures are a host of more complex animals—Gullivers in this Lilliputian realm—although most are too small to be seen by the unaided human eye, and many of the remainder are only a few millimeters in size. Among them are translucent arrowworms, tiny shrimplike creatures with one eye, snails with wings that paddle through the water, hydrozoans that grow like moss on shallow bottoms, and jellyfish that form colonies and drift like aimless sailboats on the surface.

Despite the name our land-bound ancestors gave it, earth is almost three quarters water. Although it is conventionally divided into oceans as well as into seas, bays and gulfs along the fringes, the sea itself is actually one vast encircling body of brine—an estimated 330 million cubic miles of it. By no means, of course, are microorganisms found only in vast tracts of water. Some live in the fluids of the human body. Many of these are benign; others, like the syphilis spirochete and the tuberculosis bacillus, are baneful. This volume, however, will concentrate only on those less visible denizens of the earth's salt and fresh waters, many of which form the basis of the food chain and as such are the primary source of nourishment for most living creatures, including human beings.

The sea is a relatively benevolent place for animals and plants to live, and conditions there surpass those prevailing on land in several important respects. Temperatures in the sea are less variable than they are on land; the sea provides a support against the pull of gravity for the organisms that live in it; and there is an ever-present supply of water available from which marine organisms can extract the oxygen and carbon dioxide, the minerals and salts they need. Fresh water provides a somewhat harsher environment than salt

In a 19th Century slide preparation (right), a group of diatom tests are decoratively arranged. Victorian biologists, entranced by the beauty their microscopes revealed, could not resist constructing such designs.

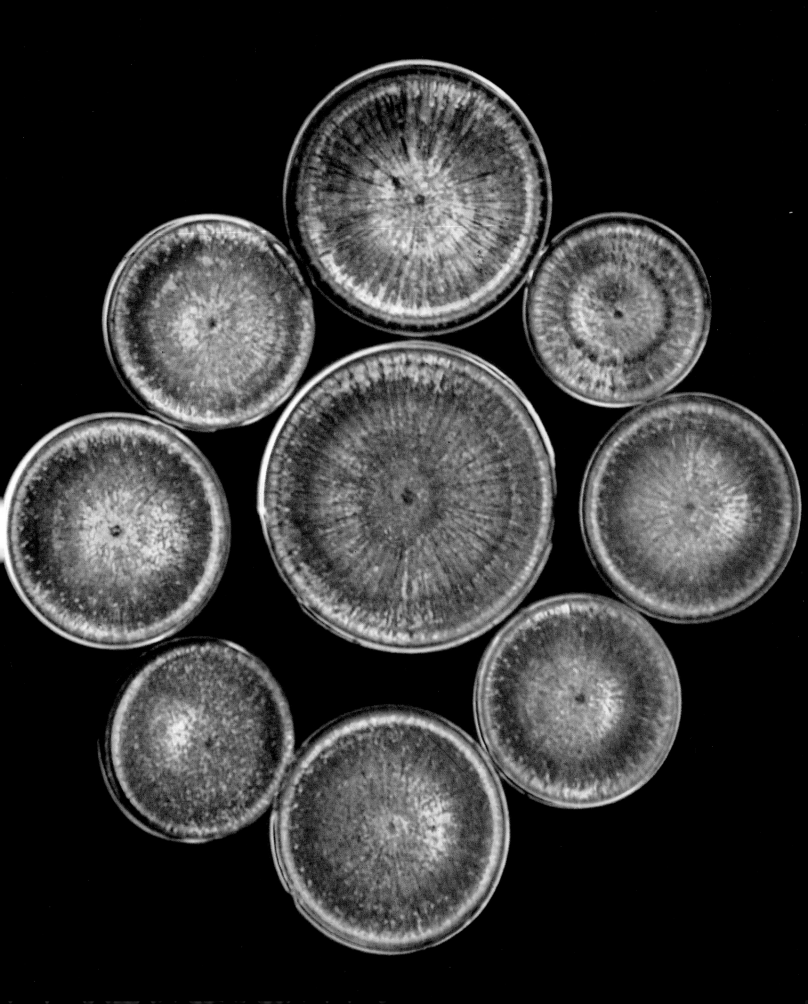

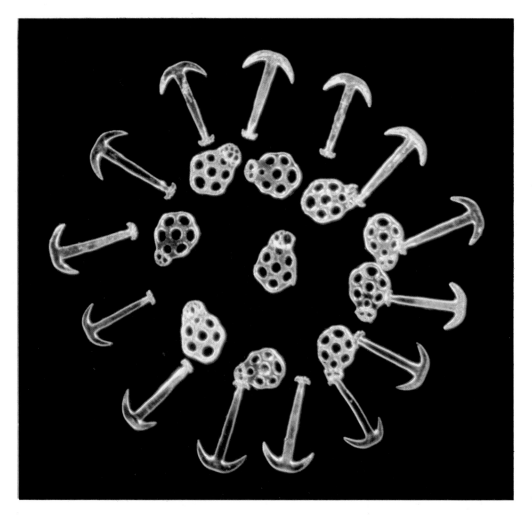

In this 19th Century slide preparation, unknown scientists delicately arranged two types of calcareous ossicles, taken from sea cucumbers, in a formal pattern. In the closeup of a surface area of a sea cucumber at right, the ossicles, in the animal's skin, are visible in their natural state. Taxonomists identify the various kinds of sea cucumber by the shape of the ossicles.

water. Salt water has about the same density as protoplasm, the material that constitutes the cells of all living creatures. Fresh water, on the other hand, lacking the salts that are present in the sea, is less dense than protoplasm. Thus, when a living organism is placed in a freshwater environment, the immediate tendency is for fresh water to permeate its outer membranes in an attempt to equalize the density. Freshwater animals must therefore wage a constant battle to maintain their own body pressure against the invasion of fluid from their environment; in this fight, most have developed special organs called contractile vacuoles, which are concerned primarily with eliminating excess fluid. This anatomical adaptation, in addition to others, has permitted life in the world's fresh waters to proliferate as it does in the sea, although with less diversity.

In water, as on land, plants are the primary source of food. The most visible and familiar aquatic plants, such as the seaweeds, comprise only a minor part—about 1 percent—of the total vegetable food supply in the ocean. The rest is made up of inestimable numbers of microscopic specks so small and weightless that they float in the water like a fine dust. The living motes make

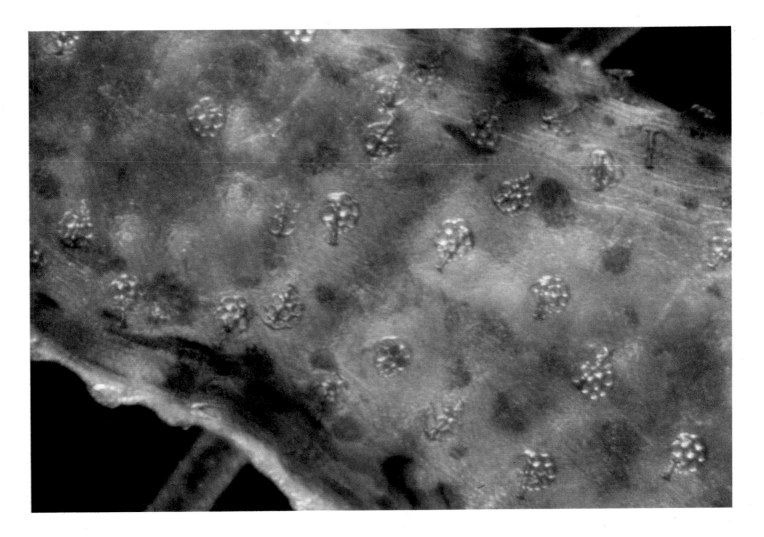

up much of what is called the plankton. Plankton—the name is derived from a Greek word that means "that which is made to wander"—includes all organisms, plant and animal, that are too small to direct their own movements over relatively long distances and are transported by the currents. They are differentiated from creatures, called the nekton, that are strong enough to swim and migrate at will, such as fish. There are times, however, when the line between plankton and nekton is somewhat indistinct. For example, when fish are in their larval stage, or when they are still very young and too weak to combat the currents, they are considered part of the plankton and remain so until they mature and grow stronger.

The wide variety of organisms that are included in the plankton are divided into two groups: the plants, or phytoplankton, and the animals, or zooplankton. Equipped with cell parts called chloroplasts that contain the green pigment chlorophyll, the members of the phytoplankton are able to use solar energy to perform photosynthesis, the life-sustaining transformation of carbon dioxide and water into sugars and starches. They are as capable of performing this task in their watery environs as are their leafy relatives on the land. Floating like bits of dust in a shaft of sunlight, these planktonic forms are abundant throughout the uppermost layers of the water, where they can absorb the maximum sunlight. Indeed, they perform 80 percent of all photosynthesis and are the main replenishers of the earth's oxygen.

The major portion of the phytoplankton is made up of one-celled algal forms, the diatoms, each enclosed in a transparent silica case, and the plant-like dinoflagellates. The latter have tiny filaments with which they beat a path through the water, but they also have chloroplasts and can manufacture their own food by means of photosynthesis. Although they contain chlorophyll, dinoflagellates are not green, but are red or brown because of the presence of additional pigments; when they occur in large numbers, dinoflagellates can tint the waters red for miles. They gave the Red Sea its name and are responsible for the noxious red tide that often forms along seacoasts during warm weather. Diatoms and dinoflagellates proliferate at that time of year because winter storms have churned up the ocean, letting the nutrient-rich bottom waters well up to the surface. The return of the warming rays of the sun in early spring sparks a resurgence of life even more impressive than the greening of a parched prairie quenched by a summer storm. With light and nutrients, the

A drop of water under a microscope (below) reveals abundant life. Often one type of organism dominates a plankton sample; the animals visible here are copepods. So small and flat are many of the transparent creatures seen under a microscope that, like the mantis shrimp larva shown at right, they could almost pass through the eye of a needle.

phytoplankters start to reproduce, each dividing every 18 to 36 hours, and in a fortnight their numbers may increase 10,000-fold. This "bloom" is immediately followed by an equally dramatic outburst of animal life, as rapidly reproducing zooplankters gorge themselves on the algae.

Within a few days or weeks, however, these lush pastures quickly become overgrazed, and reproductive activities slow down. Then in fall, when the sun still rides high in the sky, cooler, brisker winds once again stir the sea, and there is another, briefer period of intense reproduction before winter sets in.

Although representing hundreds of species, phytoplankters are almost ex-

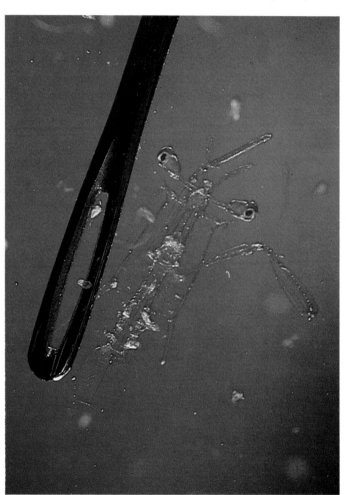

clusively tiny one-celled floaters. It is in the zooplankton that nature has shown its more extravagant flair for diversity. With members that hail from nearly every phylum of the animal kingdom, the zooplankton numbers among its permanent members creatures ranging from the simplest single-celled animals, known as protozoa, to complex crustaceans that look like miniature lobsters. Unlike phytoplankters, which are dependent on the sun's rays, zooplankters are not confined to the upper strata of the sea; they have found niches at lower depths where they feast on the rain of nutritious organic debris—composed of dead plankton and parts of larger animals—that continually falls from above.

Despite this diversity, zooplankters share many traits. Most are lightweight, with a density only slightly greater than water, which enables them to keep from sinking. Most have also developed seaworthy shapes—here a flattened, easily buoyed body, there a profusion of projections that help the animals float through the water like thistledown through the air. For the same reasons, many have long feathery appendages or flat paddle-like limbs and tails. Protective coloration enables nearly all zooplankters to blend with their environment—which means, in the case of those living near the surface of the water, that they are transparent, which makes most members of this fanciful underwater menagerie look like objects in a gallery of miniature figurines made of glass.

Considering their often almost infinitesimal size and the vastness of the sea, the numbers of plankton are incalculable, the greatest aggregate of life in the world. A quart of water can contain thousands of planktonic organisms in lean times, many times that in more favorable seasons. Attempting simply to write down their numbers, wrote Sir Alister Hardy, a noted British plankton specialist, "would wear out the nought on a typewriter." But some indication of the awesome size of their population can be gained from the immense deposits

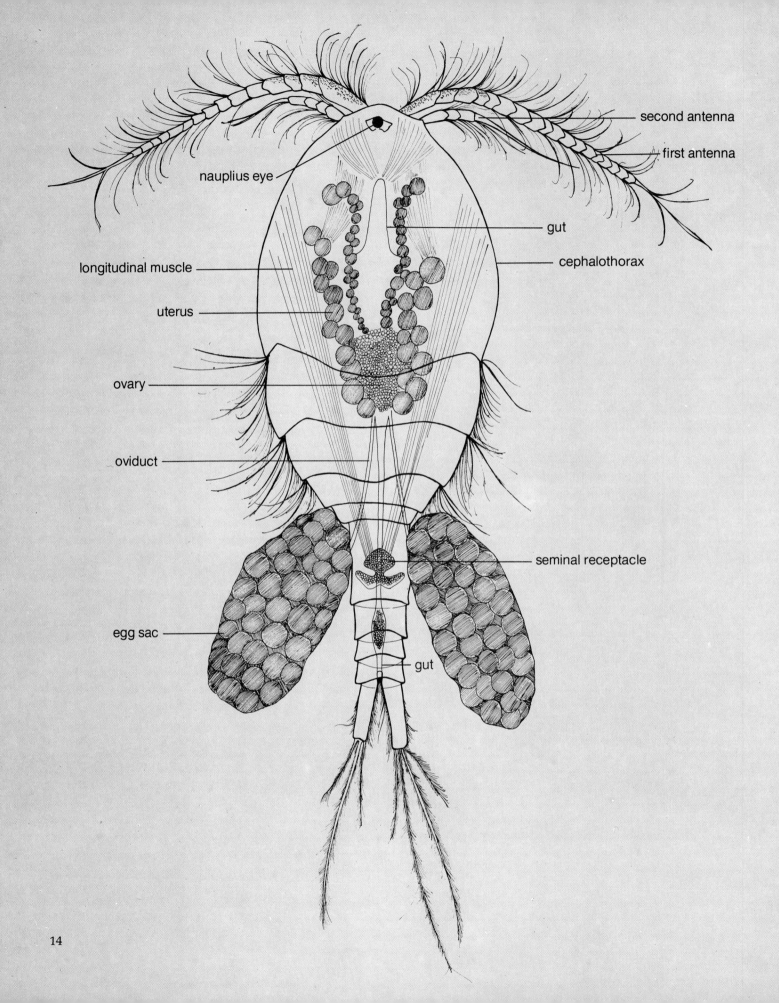

second antenna

first antenna

nauplius eye

gut

longitudinal muscle

cephalothorax

uterus

ovary

oviduct

seminal receptacle

egg sac

gut

14

of the discarded shells of dead organisms that have gradually built up over millions of years. In many places, these fossil remains, which collected eons ago on the bottoms of ancient seas, are now part of the land, and each square inch contains up to 50 million shell particles. Major contributors to these sediments are the unicellular organisms such as Coccolithophorid flagellates and Foraminifera; the chalky shells of these animals are responsible for some of the world's most spectacular accumulations of limestone—among them the famous White Cliffs of Dover in England. The glassy cases of the diatoms have also created impressive deposits of diatomaceous earth; one such deposit covers hundreds of acres in California, where it is mined by the ton to produce diatomite, a substance that is used in paints, polishes, insulation and filters. It is even frequently used in toothpaste.

Planktonic animals have some curious characteristics. One of the most baffling is the phenomenon known as vertical migration. Nearly all planktonic animals spend the night near the surface of the water grazing on phytoplankton. Then, with the first light of dawn, they retreat to deeper water, where they remain for the duration of the day, only to return to the surface again at dusk. This daily commute often covers a distance of 1,000 or more feet, and one little crustacean, barely the size of a grain of rice, was recorded hectically making the trip at speeds of up to 100 feet an hour.

When these animals arrive at the surface at night, they exhibit an even more puzzling phenomenon: bioluminescence. These eerie displays of cool, phosphorescent light are produced by members of many planktonic groups, including the tiny one-celled *Noctiluca*, or "night lights," glimmering jellyfish of all sizes and pinhead-sized crustaceans. Since these often-microscopic organisms are quickest to emit light when agitated, creating sparkling caps on breaking waves and luminous wakes behind ships, scientists long believed that it was a physical phenomenon. The 17th Century physicist Robert Boyle suggested that bioluminescence was a chemical process, whereas Benjamin Franklin thought the cause was electrical. Bioluminescence is actually a process by which chemical energy is converted into light. It is thought that bioluminescence may serve to help camouflage the planktonic organisms that exhibit it from fish predators because the glow, when seen from below, blends with the starlit canopy of the sky. What still remains a mystery, however, is why bioluminescence does not occur among freshwater animals, since lakes, ponds, streams and marshes are frequently even more richly packed with plankton than the sea, and since these freshwater organisms also pursue the same curious habit of traveling to the surface at night.

It was in fresh water—actually that freshest of waters, rain—that the world of microscopic water dwellers was first observed. In 1676, the Dutch naturalist Anton van Leeuwenhoek took droplets of rainwater that he had allowed to stand for a few days, long enough for airborne organisms and their eggs to invade it, and examined them under his homemade single-lens microscope. In his observations (excerpted on page 17), he disclosed his amazement at finding "animalcules" 1,000 times smaller than a water flea. He even went so

In the mid-19th Century, as microscope technology became highly advanced, scientists were able to examine the internal structures of pinhead-sized— although helpfully transparent —animals like the copepod. Powerful lenses revealed the amazingly complex anatomy of many microorganisms and resulted in detailed drawings such as this, which could be preserved as records for future comparative studies.

far as to declare that some of the beings "were the most wretched creatures that I have ever seen." But it was not until the 1840s that the diminutive life in the sea began to be explored, as investigators started regularly to use finely woven tow nets, which usually consisted of a little bag made of muslin or fine silk gauze; such a net was attached to a small collecting jar to capture samples of oceanic plankton and examine it under the greatly improved microscopes of the period. The most significant of these scholars was the German physiologist and anatomist Johannes Müller, whose systematic studies attracted the attention of the scientific community to this strange new world.

Until the second half of the 19th Century it was widely believed that life could not survive below 300 fathoms—1,800 feet; the scientists reasoned that the pressure of the water, which increases at 15 pounds per square inch every 33 feet, would pulverize even an oyster. Sporadic reports of life in deep-sea dredge samples were summarily dismissed as the imaginings of cooped-up sea-weary sailors. But in 1858, indisputable evidence came from an unexpected source. Forty miles of malfunctioning submarine cable in the Mediterranean was hauled up from depths of up to 7,200 feet for repair, and its casing was encrusted with oysters, snails, corals and many smaller creatures. All doubts were then finally laid to rest after 1872 when the British research vessel HMS *Challenger* undertook an intensive three-and-a-half-year voyage to study every ocean; scientists aboard recorded life at depths up to 15,000 feet. With detailed observations of the sea's currents, life-forms and chemistry, the 50-volume report that resulted from the venture laid the foundation for oceanography as a science. The world's first marine laboratory opened in Naples, Italy, the year *Challenger* set sail, and was followed by others including those in Plymouth, England, and in Woods Hole in Massachusetts.

Today enormous advances have been made in the means and devices for sounding depths, taking sea-floor samples and capturing live specimens. Sophisticated diving equipment has allowed oceanographers to observe the ocean's denizens in their natural habitats. Even more important, improvements in microscopes have made it possible for scientists to study those life-clogged realms of diminutive creatures that are as close as the nearest pond or seashore. The development of the scanning electron microscope in the late 1960s was a tremendous step forward. Previous electron microscopes had been able to enlarge only thinly sliced sections, but the scanning electron microscope, which works much like a closed-circuit television system, revealed these little creatures as they actually look in three dimensions. Though oceanography and marine biology are sciences still in their infancies and enormous reaches remain to be explored—what they have so far revealed is nothing less than the most fascinating and unfamiliar realm of the animal kingdom.

Anton van Leeuwenhoek (above) constructed microscopes with simple parts like the metal plate below. The organism to be studied was placed on the end of the pin, and turning the screw moved the organism nearer or farther away from a lens for focusing.

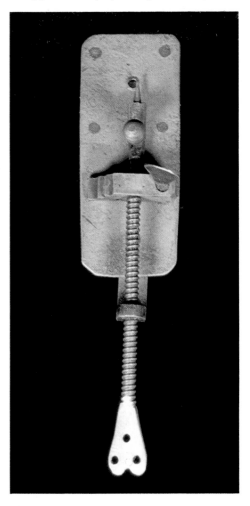

A Scientific Pioneer's Views of "Little Animals"

In 1668, the most powerful microscope then invented came to the attention of the scientists of the Royal Society of London. It was the creation of an obscure Dutch draper, Anton van Leeuwenhoek, who had constructed it as a hobby. Encouraged by the Royal Society, Leeuwenhoek spent the rest of his life developing microscopes and investigating microorganisms through the lenses. He recorded his observations in letters to the Society, and in one, written in 1677, he described the creatures to be found in a tubful of rainwater.

IN THE YEAR 1675, about half-way through September (being busy with studying air, when I had much compressed it by means of water), I discovered living creatures in rain, which had stood but a few days in a new tub, that was painted blue within. This observation provoked me to investigate this water more narrowly; and especially because these little animals were, to my eye, more than ten thousand times smaller than the animalcule which Swammerdam has portrayed, and called by the name of Water-flea, or Water-louse, which you can see alive and moving in water with the bare eye.

Of the first sort that I discovered in the said water, I saw, after divers observations, that the bodies consisted of 5, 6, 7, or 8 very clear globules, but without being able to discern any membrane or skin that held these globules together, or in which they were inclosed. When these animalcules bestirred 'emselves, they sometimes stuck out two little horns, which were continually moved, after the fashion of a horse's ears. The part between these little horns was flat, their body else being roundish, save only that it ran somewhat to a point at the hind end; at which pointed end it had a tail, near four times as long as the whole body, and looking as thick, when viewed through my microscope, as a spider's web. At the end of this tail there was a pellet, of the bigness of one of the globules of the body; and this tail I could not perceive to be used by them for their movements in very clear water. These little animals were the most wretched creatures that I have ever seen; for when, with the pellet, they did but hit on any particles or little filaments (of which there are many in water, especially if it hath but stood some days), they stuck intangled in them; and then pulled their body out into an oval, and did struggle, by stretching themselves, to get their tail loose; whereby their whole body then sprang back towards the pellet of the tail, and their tails then coiled up serpent-wise, after the fashion of a copper or iron wire that, having been wound close about a round stick, and then taken off, kept all its windings. This motion, of stretching out and pulling together the tail, continued; and I have seen several hundred animalcules, caught fast by one another in a few filaments, lying within the compass of a coarse grain of sand.

I also discovered a second sort of animalcules, whose figure was an oval; and I imagined that their head was placed at the pointed end. These were a little bit bigger than the animalcules first mentioned. Their belly is flat, provided with divers incredibly thin little feet, or little legs, which were moved very nimbly, and which I was able to discover only after sundry great efforts, and wherewith they brought off incredibly quick motions. The upper part of their body was round, and furnished inside with 8, 10, or 12 globules: otherwise these animalcules were very clear. These little animals would change their body into a perfect round, but mostly when they came to lie high and dry. Their body was also very yielding: for if they so much as brushed against a tiny filament, their body bent in, which bend also presently sprang out again; just as if you stuck your finger into a bladder full of water, and then, on removing the finger, the inpitting went away. Yet the greatest marvel was when I brought any of the animalcules on a dry place, for I then saw them change themselves at last into a round, and then the upper part of the body rose up pyramid-like, with a point jutting out in the middle; and after having thus lain moving with their feet for a little while, they burst asunder, and the globules and a watery humour flowed away on all sides, without my being able to discern even the least sign of any skin wherein these globules and the liquid had, to all appearance, been inclosed; and at such times I could discern more globules than when they were alive. This bursting asunder I figure to myself to happen thus: imagine, for example, that you have a sheep's bladder filled with shot, peas, and water; then, if you were to dash it apieces on the ground, the shot, peas, and water would scatter themselves all over the place.

Furthermore, I discovered a third sort of little animals, that were about twice as long as broad, and to my eye quite eight times smaller than the animalcules first mentioned: and I imagined, although they were so small, that I could yet make out their little legs, or little fins. Their motion was very quick, both roundabout and in a straight line.

The fourth sort of animalcules, which I also saw a-moving, were so small, that for my part I can't assign any figure to 'em. These little animals were more than a thousand times less than the eye of a full-grown louse (for I judge the diameter of the louse's eye to be more than ten times as long as that of the said creature), and they surpassed in quickness the animalcules already spoken of. I have divers times seen them standing still, as 'twere, in one spot, and twirling themselves round with a swiftness such as you see in a whip-top a-spinning before your eyes; and then again they had a circular motion, the circumference whereof was no bigger than that of a small sand-grain; and anon they would go straight ahead, or their course would be crooked.

Single-celled Sea Life

In the world of living beings no group of creatures is further removed from the realm of ordinary human experience than the sea's single-celled inhabitants. Not only are most of these beings so minuscule that their intricate structure can be observed only with the aid of a high-powered microscope, but their numbers are so great that they stagger the imagination. To the mind in search of some clear-cut, familiar distinctions to use as guideposts for an excursion through the strange universe of single-celled creatures, it may be even more perplexing to find that it is frequently difficult to differentiate between the plants and animals among them.

Even those one-celled microorganisms that can be plainly identified as plants take on unexpected forms. The commonest of these planktonic algae, as they are collectively called, are the diatoms, the primary link in the sea's organic food chain. Diatoms come packaged in tiny crystalline cases made, like glass, of silica, and they are shaped like pillboxes—their tops and bottoms slip neatly together. These shells may be round, oval or rectangular; some are shaped like pendants, others like lenses, still others like needles or stars. Some even join together in chains that look like fanciful fairyland versions of necklaces and bracelets. Examined under a high-magnification microscope, these little plants seem even more jewel-like. The surfaces of the shells are decorated with fine grooves, pits and pores that create intricate and delicate designs, and inside these cases there are shimmering strands of living protoplasm dotted with amber-colored specks. These clumps of pigment, called chloroplasts, are brown or brownish green rather than the familiar bright green of land plants' chloroplasts, and like those of their terrestrial relatives they enable the diatom to use the sun's energy to convert gases and minerals into food, the process known as photosynthesis.

Even more fascinating than these true plants, however, are the flagellates. These curious little creatures are claimed both by botanists as part of the ocean's flora and by zoologists as part of its fauna. The commonest of these little organisms are the often-luminescent dinoflagellates. Some dinoflagellates brave the open waters as delicate, unsheathed bits of protoplasm, but most are protected by mosaic-like shells of cellulose that resemble disks, acorns, or bent needles.

Like the diatoms, most of these creatures have chloro-plasts and spend the better part of their lives near the surface of the water basking in the sun. Otherwise, their lifestyle is much like that of animals. Equipped with two long whiplike appendages—the flagella from which they take their name—dinoflagellates beat their way quickly and often erratically through the surface waters. One common type, *Peridinium*, which uses one whip extending from its side to rotate itself round and round as another whip in its tail propels it forward, literally screws itself through the sea. Most dinoflagellates also have a primitive eye—a light-sensitive red spot that enables them to tell whether they are moving toward or away from the sun's life-giving rays. Some even supplement the nourishment they receive through photosynthesis by capturing and digesting smaller organisms, while others, having lost their chloroplasts, have completely crossed over into the animal kingdom.

These emigrants from the plant kingdom are clearly protozoans, which means "first animals," and they share the open seas with two other groups of protozoans—the foraminifers and the radiolarians. Unlike their amorphous freshwater and marine cousin *Amoeba*, both of these unicellular seafarers are outfitted with sturdy frames. In some bottom-dwelling foraminifers, the shell is hard and chalky, made of bits of sand and pulverized shell cemented together. Most foraminifers, however, form their cases by secreting calcium carbonate that they extract from the minerals present in the water.

The shells of the foraminifers, whose name means "hole bearers," are frequently perforated with fine pores. Thin strands of protoplasm extrude from these pores, branching and crisscrossing to form a living net. Any smaller organism that has the misfortune of drifting into this sticky web is consumed on the spot by the strands, which gather to cover the morsel and start to secrete digestive juices.

Cousins of the foraminifers, the radiolarians are among the sea's most delicately beautiful animals. Radiolarian means "rayed one," and the combination shell and skeleton that radiolarians forge out of clear silica usually has long needle-like spines. Like the foraminifers, radiolarians also extend long filaments of protoplasm to catch food—diatoms, copepods and other protozoans—but instead of forming a net, each strand stands alone. When a prey touches one, however, another immediately joins the attack, and the two adhere to the victim, trap it and then carry it back to the central mass to be digested.

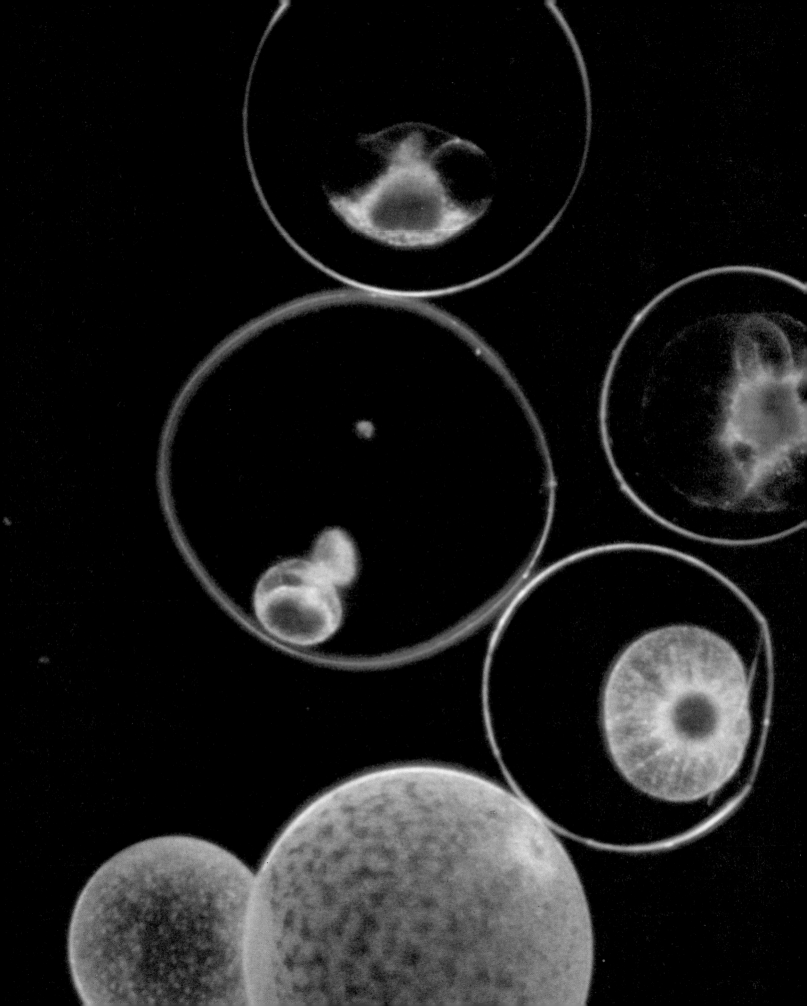

Diatoms attach themselves to branches of algae (left). One species of diatom lives anchored to copepods, often covering its hapless hosts.

Diatoms come in many shapes, but the pillbox (right) is commonest. The shell is made of silica, which diatoms extract in solution from the sea and then secrete in solid form around themselves.

Each diatom within this cluster (below) is a needle-shaped cell. The cells live stacked together like a deck of cards.

The Ocean's Grasses

Diatoms, the basic marine food plants, are so numerous and play such a vital role in the marine food chain that they have been called the "grasses of the sea." By extracting minerals from the seawater surrounding them, diatoms produce crystal shells of incredible delicacy and diversity, some of which are seen here and on the following pages. These encase the bodies of the diatoms, which are a rich source of nutrients for thousands of species of marine animals, ranging from microscopic protozoans to whales.

In order to survive such widespread predation and to maintain their numbers, diatoms reproduce at a phenomenal rate. Generally, a diatom reproduces simply by splitting in half. The top and bottom of its pillbox shell separate, each taking half the enclosed protoplasm with it. A new half shell is then secreted that fits inside the old one. If this process were repeated endlessly, however, the new diatoms would continually decrease in size and eventually die. Before they reach this point they undergo a complex series of sexual reproductive processes that restore them to their original size.

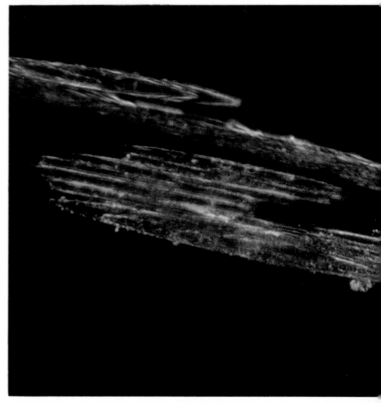

A group of diatoms link up with
one another to form a chain (right).
The brownish-yellow material
in each cell is the chlorophyll that the
tiny plant uses to manufacture food.

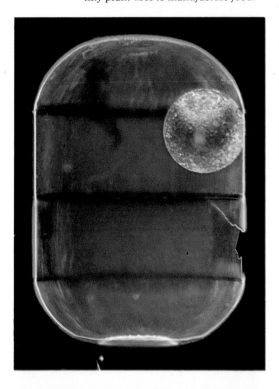

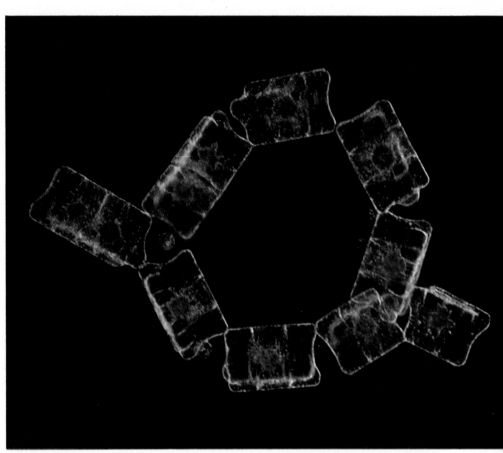

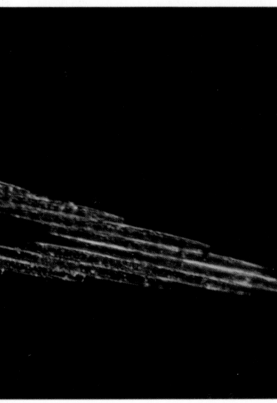

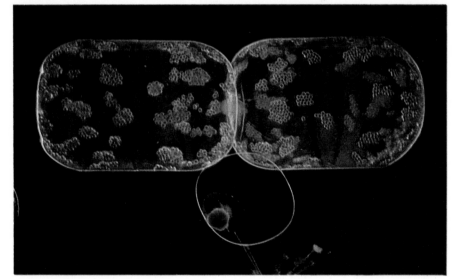

A dinoflagellate and two diatoms
(above) float together in a drop of
seawater. Diatoms are responsible
for almost all marine photosynthesis.

When diatoms die, the shells
that surround them (overleaf)
sink to the bottom and form
deposits that may be up to 700
feet thick, and are known as
diatomaceous earth.

21

Hundreds of luminescent noctilucas crowd together, giving off a ghostly ripple of light. To produce this light Noctiluca mixes luciferin and luciferase—the same chemicals that combine to make a firefly glow.

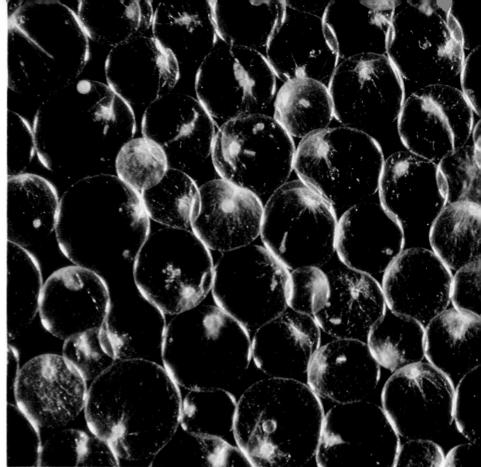

A parasitic dinoflagellate hangs onto a foraminifer (below), absorbing its food from the body of its host.

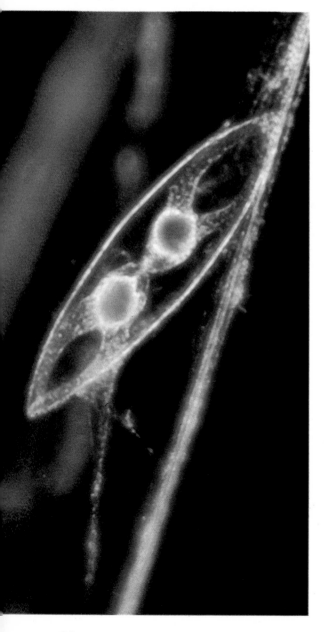

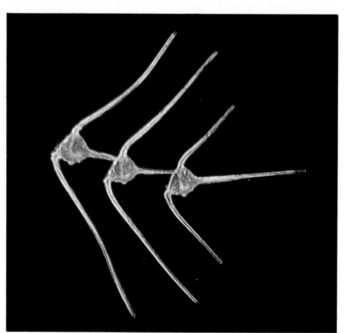

This chain of three Ceratium dinoflagellates (above) results from transverse fission, a form of asexual reproduction.

A dinoflagellate divides (right). In 25 consecutive divisions one dinoflagellate can give rise to 33 million offspring.

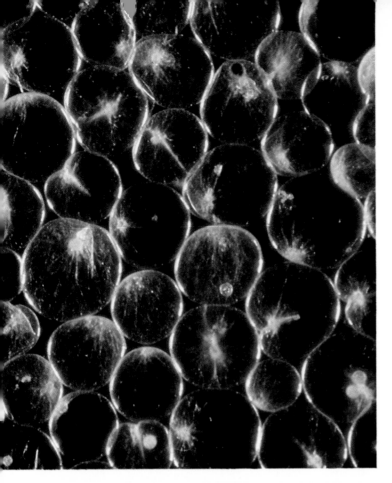

A Confusion of Roles

Flagellates are unique among unicellular organisms in that some individuals are like plants, others are like animals, and some have characteristics of both. The dinoflagellates possess two flagella—long, thin extensions that propel the organisms by means of lashing motions—and many dinoflagellates are bioluminescent. The best-known bioluminescent species is *Noctiluca*, a pinhead-sized colorless individual that glows in the dark if disturbed. It feeds chiefly on diatoms, but also eats such animals as young copepods, seizing them with a tentacle-like extension of the cell.

Some of the commonest dinoflagellates belong to the genus *Ceratium*, whose members are shaped like miniature anchors; different species can be distinguished from one another by the length of their spines. In general the tropical dinoflagellates have longer spines than those of the cold-water dinoflagellates. Objects sink more quickly in warm water than in cold, and having longer extensions maintains the tropical species near the surface, where they must be to find the phytoplankton they feed on and the sunlight they need for photosynthesis.

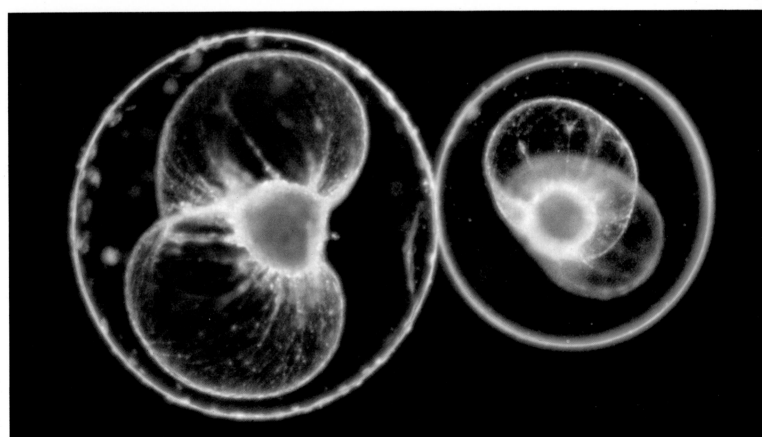

Foraminifers vary greatly in size and shape. The giant Globigerinella, seen trapping tiny crustaceans (left), can be two inches in diameter and has long spines. But most foraminifers are microscopic and live in nautilus-like multichambered shells (below).

Dressed Up in Chalk

Foraminifers can be found almost everywhere in the sea, floating in the open water or, like the vast majority, moving across the ocean bottom. Foraminifers are marine counterparts of freshwater amoebas. Unlike amoebas, however, the foraminifer's protoplasm is contained within a shell of calcium carbonate—which resembles chalk or limestone. In some foraminifers the shell expands continuously with the growth of the animal. Others secrete a succession of larger chambers that follow a symmetrical pattern as they grow, eventually creating shells that have chambers, each with a distinct shape and arrangement.

In some, the chambers are arranged in a straight line that resembles a strand of graduated beads. Others often have new chambers that form in spirals around the old ones so that the shell resembles a snail shell. Still other foraminifers successively secrete new chambers that completely surround their old ones, creating shells with onionlike layers. Most foraminiferan shells have many small pores through which protoplasm can stream out and form pseudopodia that enable the animals to move and trap food.

Naturally Ornate

The silica-shelled radiolarians are close relatives of the amoebas and the foraminifers, but unlike their chalk-shelled, bottom-loving foraminiferan cousins, the radiolarians are most numerous in the upper 650 feet of the ocean. The radiolarian's body is usually spherical and is divided into an inner and an outer part. The inner part, called the central capsule, contains one or more nuclei and is surrounded by a membrane. The membrane contains perforations through which the cytoplasm of the central capsule merges with that of the outer part of the animal's body, forming a broad layer that surrounds the central cap-sule. Within this outer layer are large numbers of dino-flagellates that live symbiotically with their radiolarian host, as well as numerous vacuoles that are filled with fluid and give the cytoplasm a frothy appearance.

Almost all radiolarians have skeletons. Some are made up of long, needlelike spines that extend out from the central capsule beyond the outer surface of the body. Others are in the form of a lattice sphere arranged concentrically around the radiolarian. There may be any number of such spheres inside and outside the body, and some radiolarians have a combination of both types.

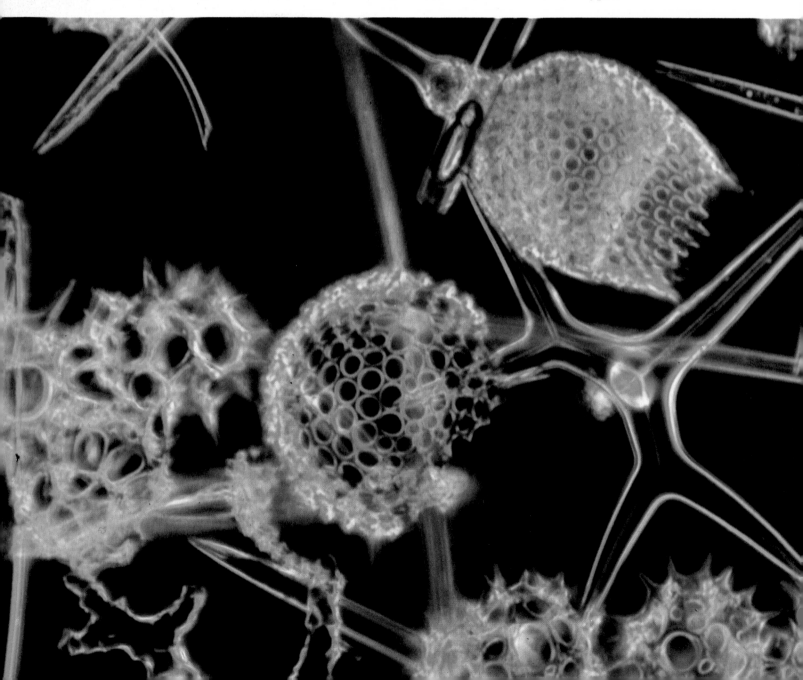

The shells of most radiolarians are made up of transparent silica, and both the spined species (right) and those whose skeletons look like latticework (below) are the most delicate of all marine zooplankton.

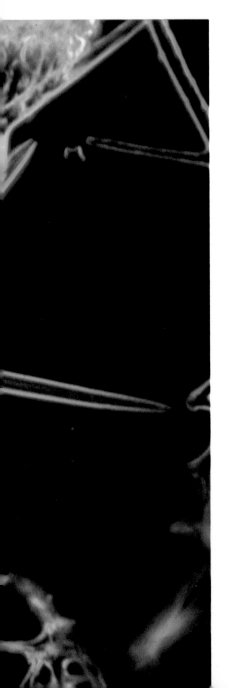

The Center of Life

by L. L. Larison Cudmore

A leading molecular biologist, L. L. Larison Cudmore has taught at the University of Massachusetts and at Boston University. In this excerpt from her book called The Center of Life *she pays a lyrical tribute to some single-celled water dwellers.*

It is safe to say that, as a group, the protists do not form an integral part of the American consciousness. The amoeba is the only one that has achieved much media recognition. Its name is used as a pejorative synonym for anyone without personality, suspected of leading a spineless, creeping kind of existence; and the threat of amoebic dysentery keeps travelers wary of the local water supply. We are both slandering the amoeba and missing a lot, including some very poetic names: *Chaos chaos* (with a name like that, it's *bound* to be interesting); *Acinetopsis rara; Ephilota gemmipara; Gonyaulax polyhedra; Noctiluca; Stentor ceruleus.* The names don't exactly spill trippingly off our tongues like the syllables of Lolita off the tongue of Humbert Humbert; but they are beautiful, and so are the namesakes. Not as beautiful as some nymphets, perhaps, but what nymphet can glow with a cold mysterious blue-green fire like *Noctiluca*, igniting Pacific or Atlantic waves into glorious fireworks? *Noctiluca* (nightlight) is luminescent, lighting up the marine night, the source of phosphorescence in the ocean. *Stentor*, after the trumpet-voiced herald in the *Iliad*, is a large vivid-blue trumpet, with waving fringes around its bell. Though attached by a stalk to any surface, if it is annoyed by taps of a pencil, it will first contract; just as anyone else would hunch his shoulders and pull his neck down into them. If repeatedly annoyed, *Stentor* will loose its hold and indignantly swim away; rather complicated behavior for a single cell with no nerves and no brain. But even the blue trumpets of *Stentor* are not the most interesting denizens of this wild and beautiful Lilliput world, half Disney, half Dali.

Primitive Freshwater Life

Although many people might imagine that the earth's freshwater basins and streams are more hospitable to life than are the vast oceans, the opposite is true. To the diminutive creatures that live in them, bodies of fresh water offer a harsher life than does the sea, because they lack the salinity that is so closely akin to the chemical makeup of living organisms. In addition, freshwater environments are generally less supportive of life since they are more likely to freeze over in winter.

Yet small, simple organisms have not only survived but have thrived in fresh water. The most numerous inhabitants are a number of tiny single-celled creatures that can transform the sun's energy into food. Prominent among them are diatoms, the same small plants, in hard, glassy cases, that fill the oceans. When summer fades, they are joined by their relatives the desmids, which look like little green cigars or unripe bananas encased in tough, clear cellulose shells. Also present are the flagellates, especially the pod-shaped *Euglena* and the disklike *Chlamydomonas*, both of which are pea green. These peculiar creatures are both plant and animal. Like plants, they have chloroplasts to absorb the sun's life-sustaining rays and sensitive eyespots that orient them toward the light. But like animals, they are able to wiggle through the water using their long whiplike flagella.

Flagellates are frequently gregarious, and many species live only in colonies. The most outstanding of these confederations is *Volvox*. Individuals, often numbering in the thousands, live together in a hollow gelatinous sphere that frequently becomes large enough to be seen by the naked eye as a tiny green speck rolling gracefully through the water. This floating congregation reproduces by creating a number of smaller colonies within itself. When these so-called daughter colonies leave home, the parent splits open to release them, and then, its own life cycle at an end, sinks to the bottom.

Most other one-celled freshwater inhabitants are true animals, and best known among these protozoans is one of nature's simplest life-forms—*Amoeba*. Generations of biology students have observed amoebas—little more than globs of semifluid protoplasm—engulfing prey with armlike projections that they can extend from any part of their bodies, and reproducing by simply dividing in half.

Somewhat more complex in structure is another common group of protozoans, the ciliates. Represented in their best-known form by *Paramecium*, ciliates are a diverse clan of single-celled animals characterized by the fine hairlike cilia that they use to rake in food and paddle through the water. Usually arranged in rows that beat one after the other, the cilia look, in motion, like a wheat field rippled by a sudden gust of wind.

More closely related to plants than are the parameciums are other ciliates, such as *Vorticella*, which proliferate in late-summer and autumn waters filled with the decaying matter on which they feed. Vorticellas are semisessile, a word that describes the fact that they live in movable aggregates that attach themselves to rocks or weeds; close up, they look like beds of tiny bell-shaped flowers on slender coiling stems. The stentors, which look like long hunting horns turned on end, are also semisessile. When stentors, which are versatile creatures, move in search of food, they transform themselves into globular balls for the journey. After anchoring themselves once again, they resume their elongated shape.

A scant step up the ladder toward complexity from these protozoans are another group of animals, the hydras—freshwater dwellers related to the jellyfish—which often carpet the bottoms of ponds like fine slippery moss. One quarter to one half inch in length, hydras have slender tubular bodies crowned by long, stinging tentacles for capturing prey. At a slightly higher evolutionary level are a wide variety of small worms, including the thin, soft-bodied flatworm that is the simplest of bilaterally symmetrical animals, i.e., animals with a front end and a rear, a right side and a left, and an upper and a lower surface. The rotifers, another kind of small worm, have cylindrical trunks topped with whirling disks of cilia that look like the brushes on an electric floor waxer.

The most complex—and in some ways the least known among these miniature freshwater creatures—are the crustaceans. Unlike their larger seagoing relatives, such as the lobster and the shrimp, these little animals usually have crystal-clear shells. Indeed, *Argulus*, a common fish parasite, is so transparent that it is nearly invisible as it lies flat amid the scales of its host, to which it is attached by suction cups. One of the most interesting and advanced of these minuscule crustaceans is the water flea *Daphnia*, which usually gives birth to free-swimming young whose entire embryonic development can be observed through the mother's glassy shell.

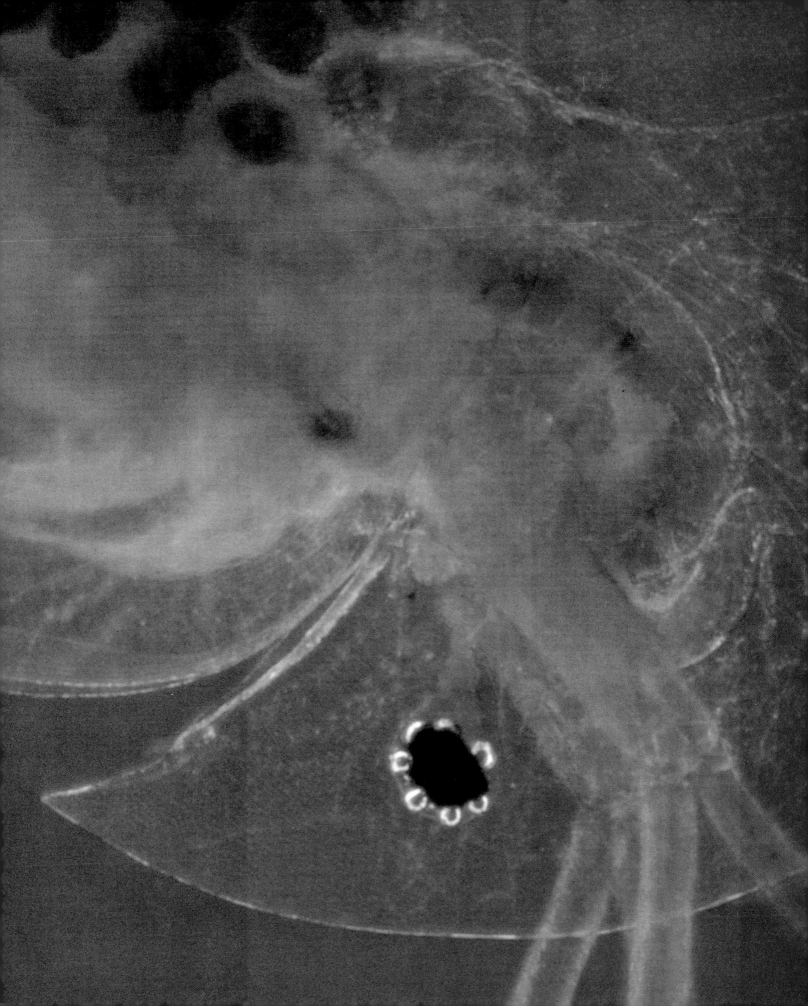

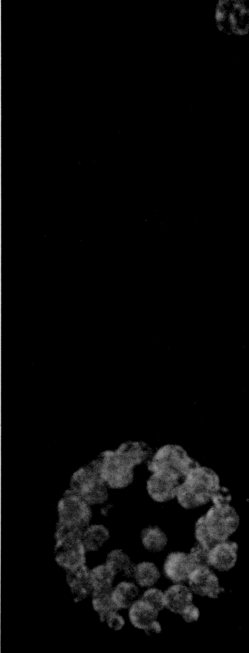

Scores of Euglena (left) collide in a droplet of water. At the base of Euglena's flagellum is an eyespot that contains a light-sensitive pigment, allowing the protozoan to orient itself and move toward the source of light.

A large Volvox colony (right, center) dwarfs four other genera of protozoans. The entire mass, called the parent colony, contains as many as 10 offspring, which are known as daughter colonies.

Plantlike Animals

The familiar pea-green scum that often coats the surfaces of freshwater ponds, especially during the summer, can usually be attributed to large populations of two microscopic protozoans, *Euglena* and *Volvox*. Both are flagellates, organisms that are distinguished by one or more hairlike extensions, called flagella, that grow from their cell covering, or pellicle. The flagella propel the organisms with rapid lashing motions.

Torpedo shaped, *Euglena* straddles the line between the plant and animal kingdoms. Like plants, it nourishes itself by means of photosynthesis, using the green pigments contained in its cell to convert the sun's energy into nutrients. When light is unavailable, however, *Euglena* is able, like an animal, to obtain food from its environment.

Volvox, also capable of photosynthesis, is made up of numerous flagellated cells embedded in the gelatinous covering of a fluid-filled sphere. The flagella of the individual cells protrude through the envelope, and the synchronized beating of these filaments moves the entire *Volvox* colony through the water.

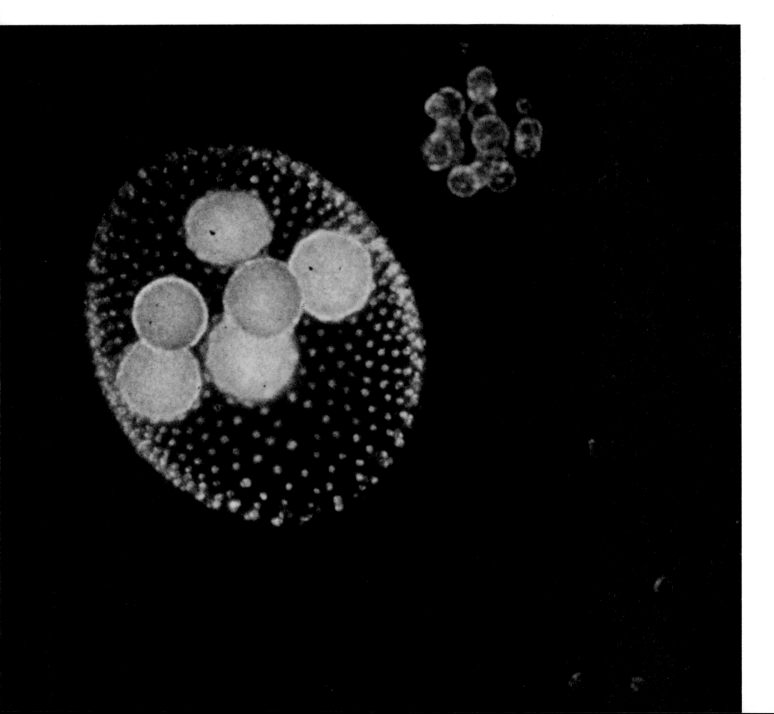

Machinery for Evolution

by Joseph Wood Krutch

A noted literary and drama critic, Joseph Wood Krutch went to live in the Arizona desert in the 1950s and, combining humanism with scientific observation, began writing about the world of nature. In this excerpt from a chapter in The Great Chain of Life *Krutch witnesses the death of a volvox through a microscope and speculates on its meaning.*

Even for the sake of picturesqueness and drama I would hesitate to say that Volvox invented Love as well as Sex. What he invented was perhaps at most only the possibility of Love. But in even the simplest creature Death—either accidental as it always is in one-celled creatures or sometimes natural as it may be in Volvox—is all too plainly like death in every other creature up to man. It is something we have not been able to change or complicate any more than we have been able to abolish it. Volvox may not love as we love, but he seems to die as we die.

A drop of water suspended in the intense beam of a microscope is not a very favorable environment for any organism, and several times I have seen a Volvox die. Usually his activity slows down and then stops. There comes the moment when he gives up his little ghost, though the body, like a human corpse, may seem hardly different from what it was before. A tiny spark is extinguished as suddenly and as irrevocably as the larger spark in any larger animal. What was alive is dead. The immeasurable, indescribable difference between the animate and the inanimate has been produced in a single instant. The spark can no more be revived in Volvox than in man. He was rounder than Humpty-Dumpty but not all the king's horses or all the king's men....

It is no wonder, I say to myself, that so many men in so many different places and at so many different times have assumed that some soul must at the moment of death fly the body and betake itself elsewhere. It is the most natural of all possible theories, even if it is not the current one. The dead body of even a Volvox seems suddenly to have been vacated. Something intangible seems to have departed from it. What, on the contrary, I do find surprising is not the assumption that men have souls, but that it should ever have come to be commonly assumed that no other creature has. The sense that something which was there is gone is almost as strong in the one case as in the other and nothing suggests that the death of one is radically different from the death of the other. The very word "inanimate" means "without a soul" and the fact that we still use it testifies to its appropriateness.

I assume that the biologists are right when they tell me that Volvox, having got as far as it did, seems to have got no farther. Perhaps some other creature independently paralleled his inventions—which would make the whole thing at least twice as remarkable.

Looking again at the Roller I console him thus: At least you were on the right track. Like many others in the history of invention, like, to take a very minor example, Langley and his airplane—you were on the right track even though something stopped you before ultimate success. Once you had transformed a colony into an integrated individual you showed how it was possible for living creatures to achieve more than merely microscopic size. Once you had invented the differentiation of the sexes you had started on the way to poetry as well as to rich variability.

It may also be true that none of your other inventions was more important than Death, without which none of the others could have been fully effective. As a certain multicellular, mortal and sexually-differentiated individual called Bernard Shaw has argued, nature would not have been able to experiment very freely with new forms if the earlier experiments were not removed after a reasonable time. The potentially immortal amoeba got nowhere. Only mortal creatures evolved.

A Simple Success

Amoeba is considered the simplest of protozoans because it has very few organelles, specialized cell parts similar to the organs of higher animals. Yet this asymmetrical, unicellular blob of cytoplasm is among the most successful forms of life. Amoebas are found all over the world, not only in fresh water, but also in oceans and in the soil—where they live on the tiny drops of moisture that are trapped between particles of dirt.

Amoeba is a member of the class of protozoans called Sarcodina, which includes animals that have flowing body extensions called pseudopodia, or false feet. In line with the name, these temporary extensions are used for locomotion, but they are also used for feeding. Encountering small particles of foods such as diatoms, other protozoans or even such multicellular organisms as rotifers and nematodes, an amoeba extends a finger-like mass of cytoplasm that surrounds the quarry, and eventually completely engulfs it within a pocket called a food vacuole, which breaks the food down into nutritious compounds that are incorporated into the amoeba's body.

Decaying vegetable matter surrounds the amoeba shown above. The long, slender, threadlike forms in the photograph are the bodies of nematode worms that share the environment.

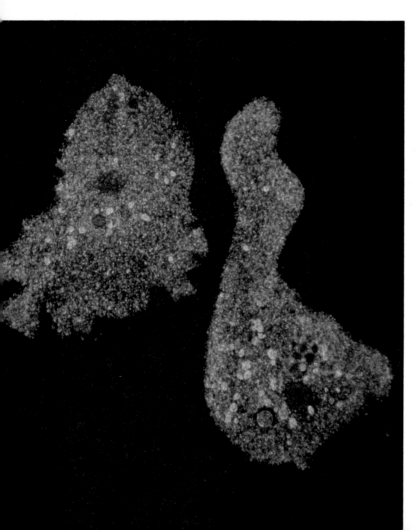

Two similar amoebas (left) are the result of binary fission, the process by which most amoebas reproduce. The offspring, called daughters, each have half of the parent's cell material.

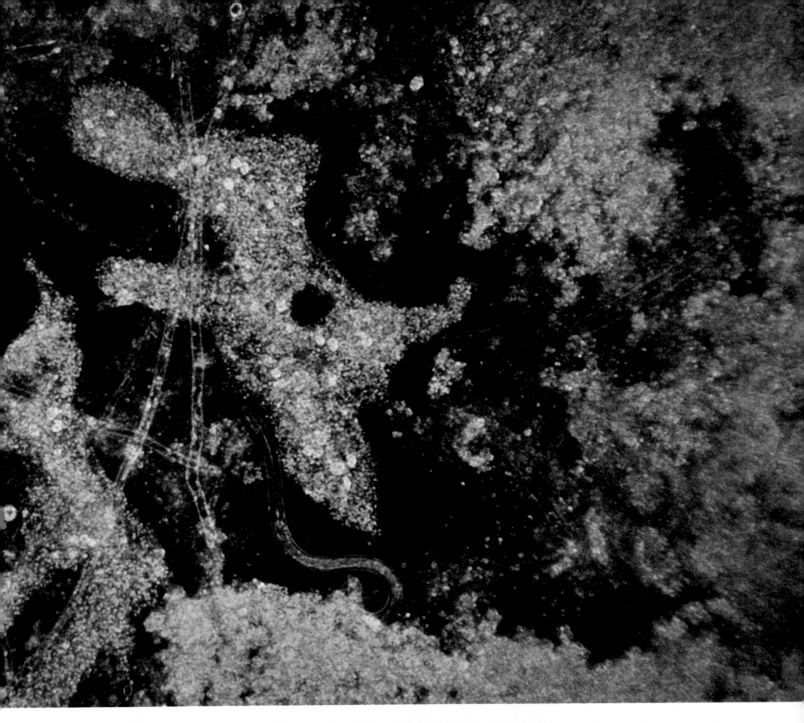

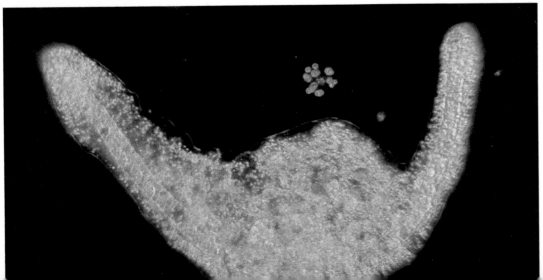

The body of an amoeba (left) is distorted by the strand of alga it has just eaten. Occasional grazers of such waterborne greenery, amoebas usually feed on small, single-celled animals such as parameciums.

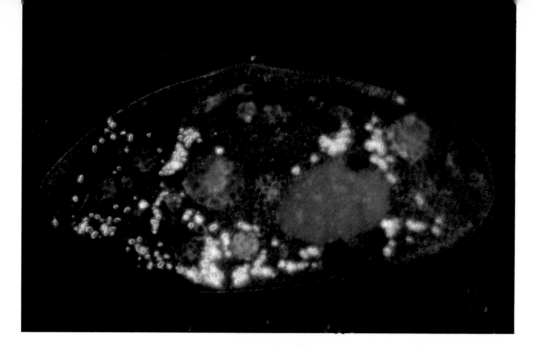

A free-swimming Stentor loses its elongated trumpet form by contracting its body into a globular shape (right). The blue beadlike chain visible within the body is the macronucleus. These beads fuse into a single mass before asexual reproduction, when the organism splits in two (far right).

Like all ciliates, Paramecium (above) has two types of nuclei: the macronucleus—light blue in this photograph—which controls the cell's day-to-day activities and is vital for normal metabolism, and one or more micronuclei—seen here as dark blue. Micronuclei store the cell's genetic information and are essential to reproduction.

Water rich in decaying plant matter provides a feast for a mass of stentors (right). The broad end of Stentor's body is rimmed by clumps of cilia called membranelles. These beat in rapid succession—always clockwise—to create a whirlpool effect that draws food-laden water to the animal's oral cavity.

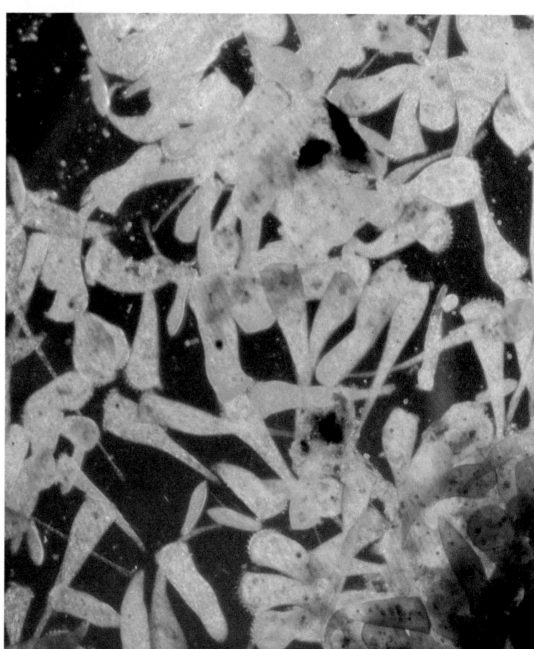

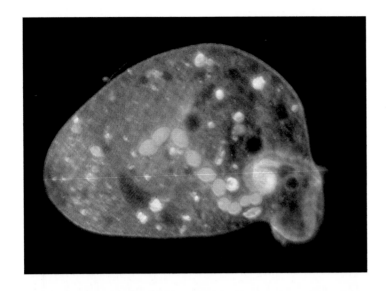

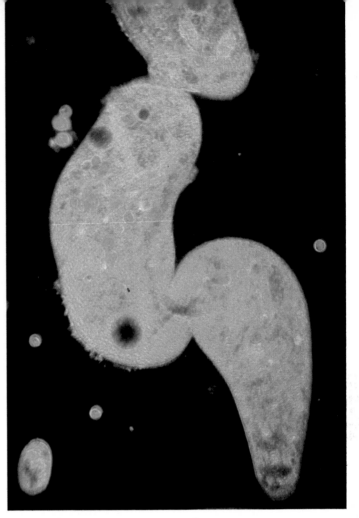

Feeders on Decay

The largest class of protozoans, with about 6,000 species, are the ciliates—those that use hairlike extensions called cilia to propel themselves or to acquire food. Cilia are similar to flagella, but are usually shorter and more numerous. Ciliates are found in large numbers in all bodies of fresh water, especially where there is abundant decaying matter; natural recyclers of waste, most of them feed on bacteria also. The most familiar ciliate is *Paramecium*, whose slipper-shaped body is surrounded by thousands of cilia. The rhythmical beating of these tiny filaments can propel a paramecium through the water at an astonishing rate.

Among the largest of the ciliates is the freshwater giant, *Stentor*, which can measure up to 3/25 of an inch in length. Named for the "bronze-voiced" Greek herald of Homer's *Iliad*, *Stentor's* body assumes a trumpet shape when it is fully extended as in feeding, when it attaches itself to a rock or plant by its holdfast, a sticky mass that the animal forms whenever it lights on an object. This provides such a secure hold that *Stentor* can stretch in all directions for food without detaching itself.

41

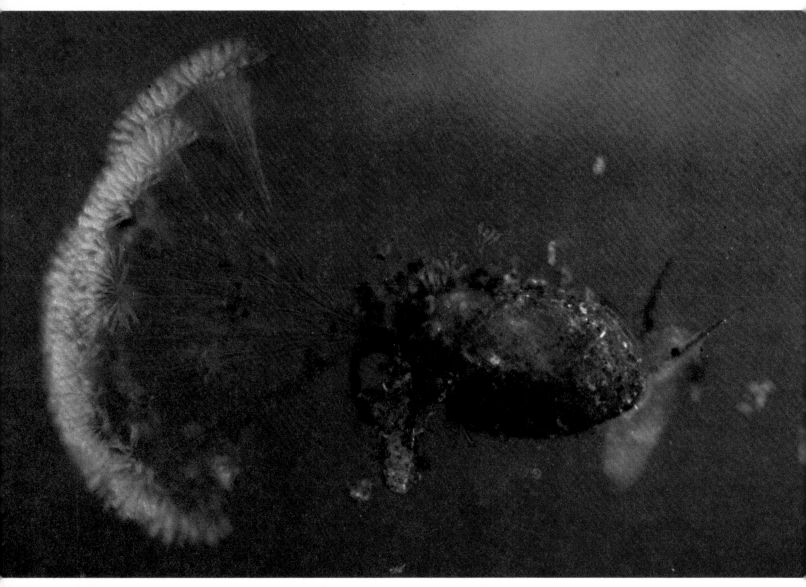

Sedentary Exceptions

Unlike the vast majority of free-swimming, solitary ciliates like *Paramecium* and the semisessile *Stentor* (pages 40-41)—such members of the class Ciliata as *Vorticella* and the colonial *Carchesium* seen on these pages live a sedentary life attached to the bottom or to a plant.

Though true ciliates, *Vorticella* and *Carchesium* have relatively few cilia, and these are confined to the edge around the feeding disk at the wide end of their typically bell-shaped bodies. The cilia adhere to one another, forming a membrane that continuously undulates, sweeping bacteria and other particles of food into the organism's mouth. This motion creates a whirlpool, or vortex, from which the genus *Vorticella* derives its name.

Vorticella and *Carchesium* spend most of their lives attached to rocks or plants, anchored by means of long slender stalks, each of which contains a spiral thread made up of fibers called myonemes. These function much like coiled springs that contract and then expand rapidly, allowing the ciliates to pop themselves loose and move on to a new anchorage.

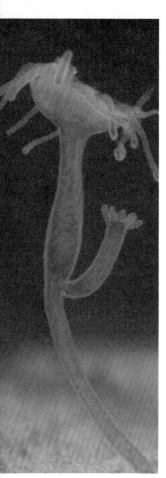

A green hydra (left) traps a copepod by means of the stinging cells, or nematocysts, lining its tentacles. The microscopic crustacean is gradually pulled into the hydra's gastrovascular cavity (left, bottom) where it will be digested.

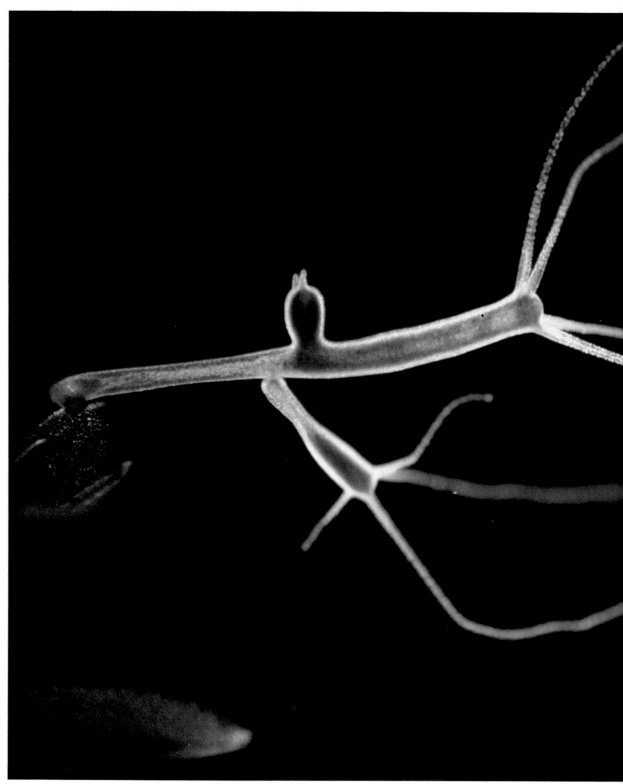

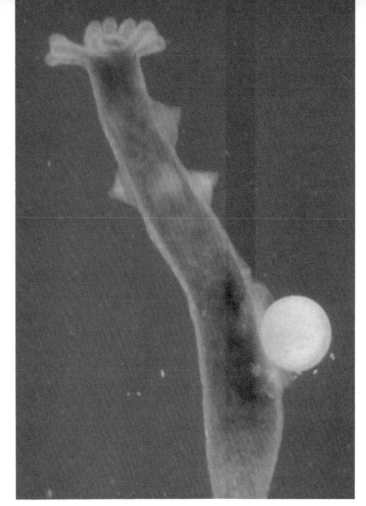

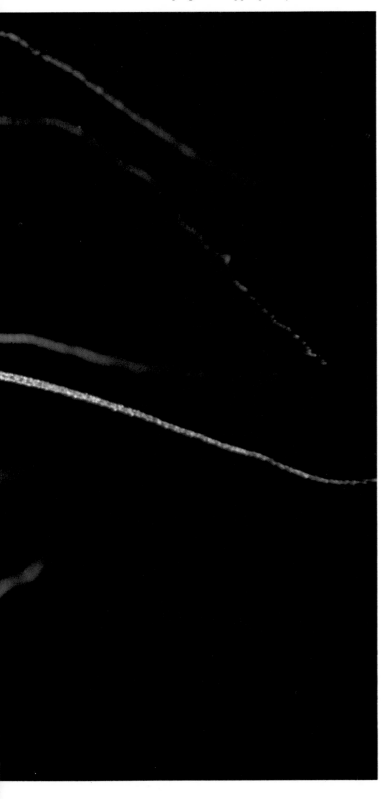

A brown hydra (below) reproduces asexually by budding. A sexually reproducing green hydra (right) is about to release a fertilized egg. A hermaphroditic species, this hydra also has testes developing on the upper part of its stalk.

The Hydras

Clean, fresh waters teem with hydras, slender polyps that live in solitary attachment to submerged rocks and vegetation. Hydras are named after the nine-headed monster slain by Hercules, and just as the mythical Hydra could not only replace a head lost in combat but also furnish two new ones, its namesake can also regenerate body parts.

Hydras employ two methods of reproduction, depending on the time of year. During spring and summer, hydras reproduce asexually by budding: A protrusion forms on the hydra's body wall, and soon a mouth, surrounded by tentacles, develops on the bud's outward end. Eventually, the bud detaches from the parent and grows into an independent organism. Hydras become sexually mature in the autumn, when ovaries or testes develop on the hydra's stalk. Ovaries contain eggs that grow steadily until they rupture the stalk's outer layer. Testes appear as conical mounds on the stalk, from which sperm escape into the water and penetrate nearby eggs. Fertilized eggs develop tough shells that protect them during the winter. In the spring the shells soften and new hydras emerge.

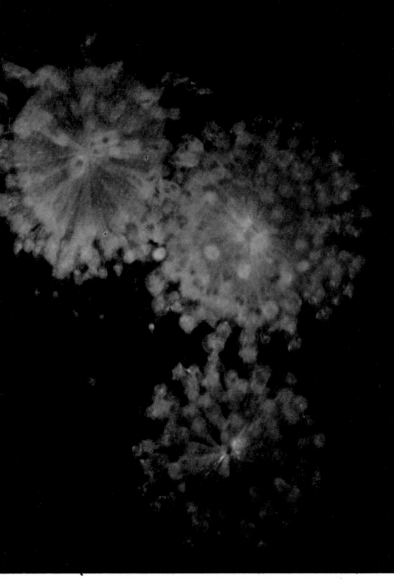

Looking like bouquets of flowers, three colonies of rotifers move together. Each member of a colony has its own means of locomotion, a corona of cilia, and their combined beat propels the entire colony.

Tubifex worms (below) form a dense cluster on the bed of a stream. These worms wave the posterior end of their bodies to create a current to bring water containing oxygen to them. When disturbed, they retreat into tunnels that they dig in the mud.

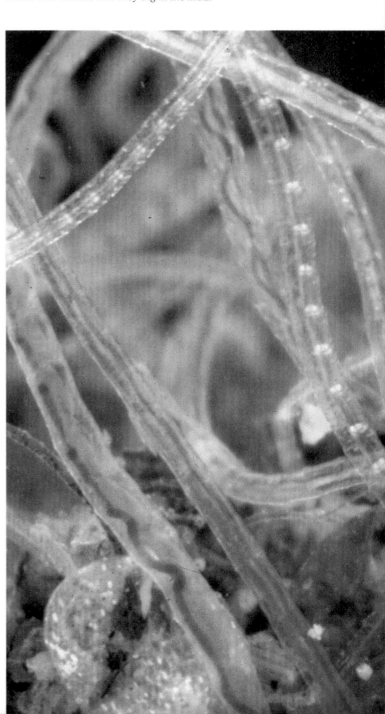

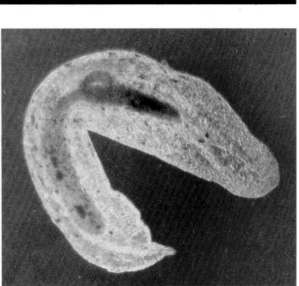

The digestive tract of a turbellarian is visible through its transparent body. The flatworm's mouth is the only opening in this system.

Primitive Symmetry

The turbellarian flatworms, members of the phylum Platyhelminthes, are the lowest animals on the evolutionary ladder to exhibit bilateral symmetry—that is, the body has definite anterior and posterior ends, left and right sides as well as ventral and dorsal sides. In their head areas these animals have their sensory organs and a mass of nerve cells that make up a kind of brain. Many turbellarians are marine, but some, like the one seen here, inhabit the bottoms of lakes, ponds, springs and streams.

Somewhat more complex are the rotifers, or wheel animalcules, whose elongated, cylindrical, transparent bodies are topped with coronas of cilia that, when beating, resemble a rotating wheel. These cilia are used for both feeding and locomotion. Most rotifers are solitary, free-swimming animals, but some are sessile and a few form colonies. Still more advanced—and probably the most familiar of all the wormlike animals—are the annelids, or segmented worms, such as *Tubifex*. Usually red or brown in color, this small worm needs very little oxygen to survive; it is found in muddy bottoms rich in organic matter.

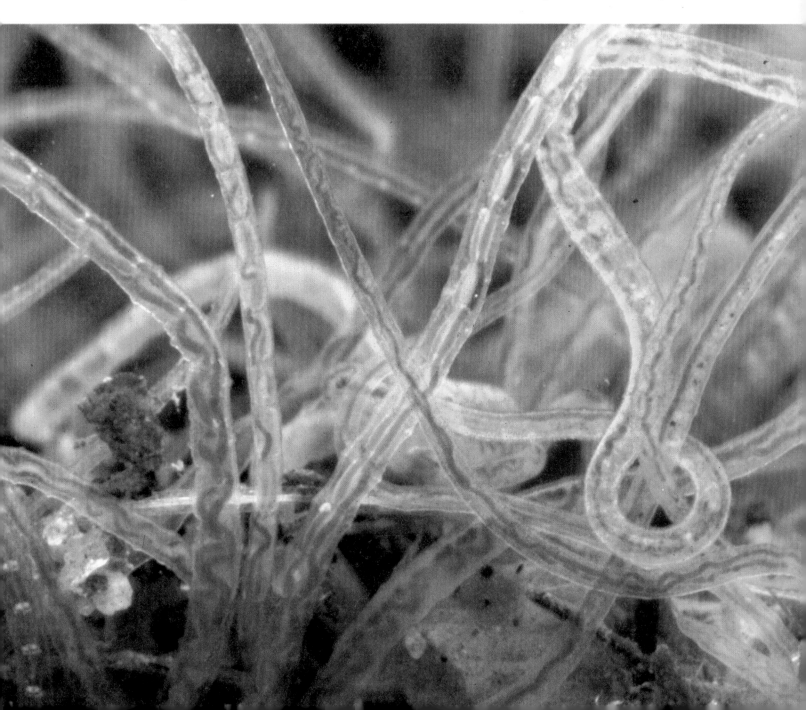

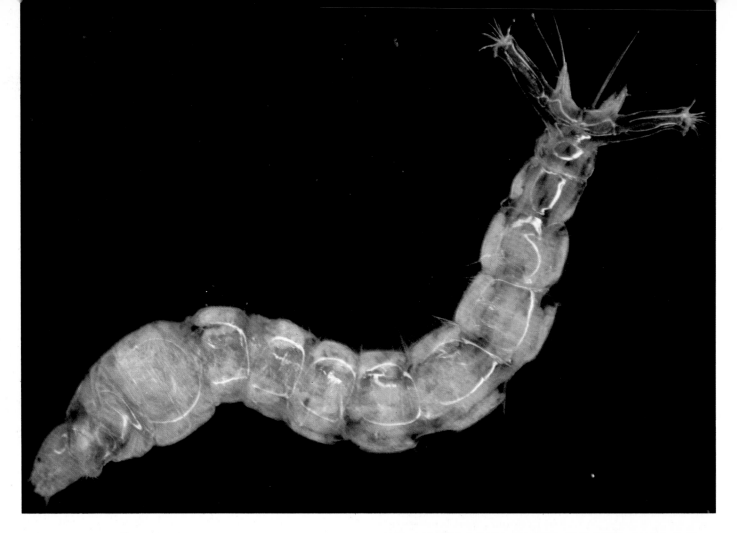

Fly Babies

The most densely populated zone of a small body of fresh water is its lower stratum. Rich in organic debris, this area is a haven for numerous creatures, including the midge larvae seen on these pages.

Adult midges are mosquito-like flies. In their pre-adult life they go through various stages of development, a process called complete metamorphosis. From eggs they develop into larvae, which eventually become pupae, the stage that gives rise to the adult form.

Midge larvae are extremely active. The larvae of *Chaoborus crystallinus*, also known as the ghost or phantom midge, are especially remarkable in being able to suspend themselves motionlessly in midwater; there they lie in wait for passing young water fleas and the larvae of other insects, which they grab with their pincerlike antennae. The phantom midge is able to control its buoyancy by regulating the gas content of the two pairs of air sacs that are located near its front and rear ends. In addition, *Chaoborus crystallinus*, is able, by bending its body in half, to reverse its position in the water.

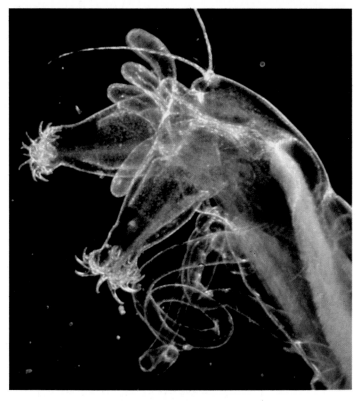

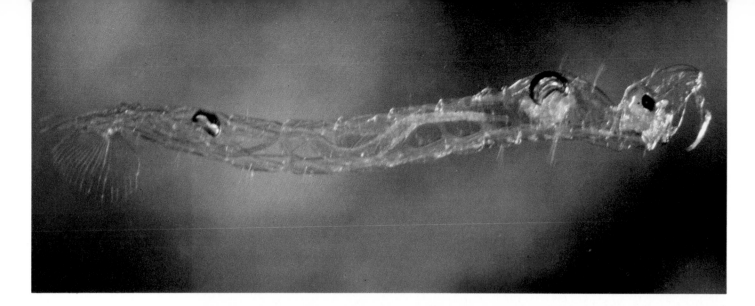

The crystal-clear body of the larva of the midge Chaoborus (above) accounts for its common name, the phantom midge. The two silvery blobs within its body are air sacs.

Fine hairs cover the body of the Tanypus midge larva (left, top). This insect develops under water in its larval stage and breathes by means of the two respiratory trumpets that project from the end of its abdomen (left, bottom).

The so-called bloodworm midge larva (right) gets its name from the color of its body fluid, which contains hemoglobin. The capacity of hemoglobin to gather oxygen allows the larva to inhabit the oxygen-sparse waters near the bottom.

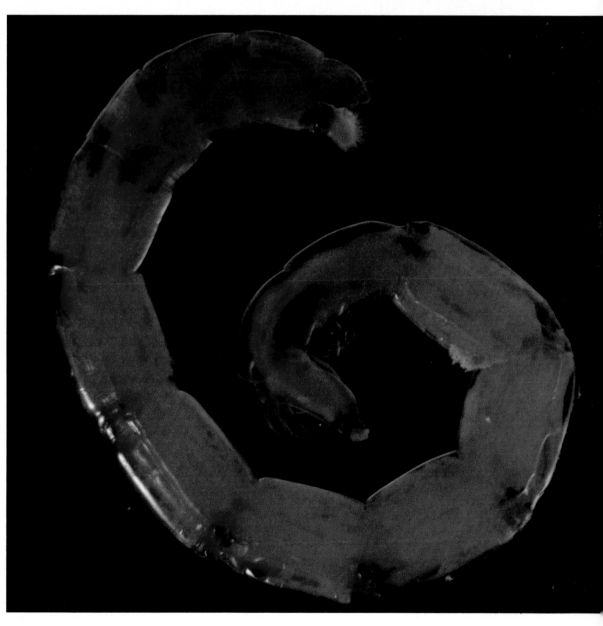

A Way to Beat the Winter

In dozens of different species, water fleas swarm in fresh water in colorful animated clouds. The most familiar is probably *Daphnia*, seen on these and the following pages.

In early spring, the *Daphnia* population is made up primarily of females. They reproduce parthenogenetically —producing offspring from unfertilized eggs, which develop in a special brood chamber located on the water flea's back. The eggs vary in number from very few to as many as 50, depending on the conditions existing in the water flea's environment. The young remain in the brood chamber for a few days after they have hatched and are then released.

Male *Daphnia* begin to appear in late spring at the same time that the females reduce egg production to only one or two eggs per clutch. These are fertilized by the male and stored in the female's brood chamber, which is now thickened and darker in color. The entire chamber is eventually released and then called an ephippium; the eggs are protected by the ephippium from freezing and drying, and are able to survive the winter, developing into adult water fleas the following spring.

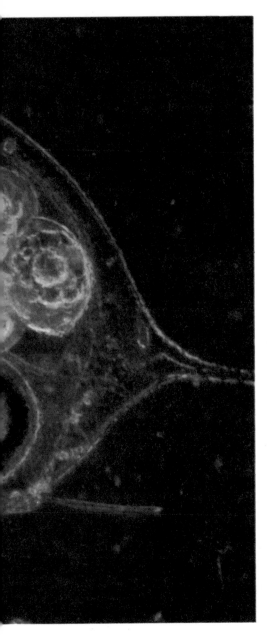

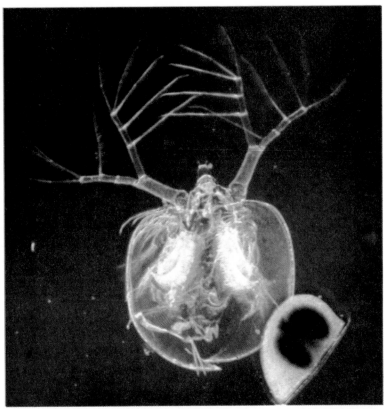

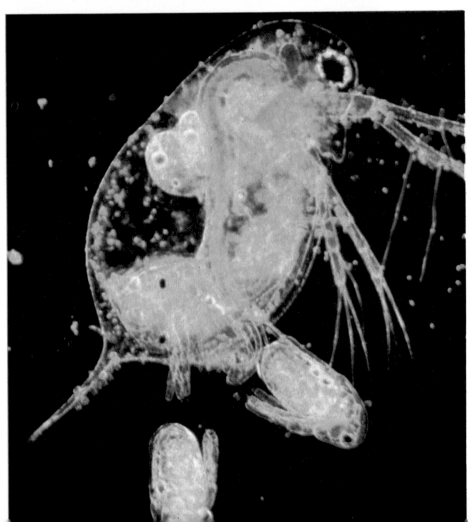

A female Daphnia (above) carries her parthenogenetic eggs in her dorsal brood chamber. When the young are released (right) they undergo several molts before being able to reproduce. When Daphnia reproduces by cross-fertilization, the ephippium containing the fertilized eggs is shed along with the rest of the exoskeleton when the female undergoes her next molt (right, top).

Summer waters of a pond blush with a burgeoning population of pink Daphnia (overleaf). These crustaceans feed by filtering microscopic algae from the water.

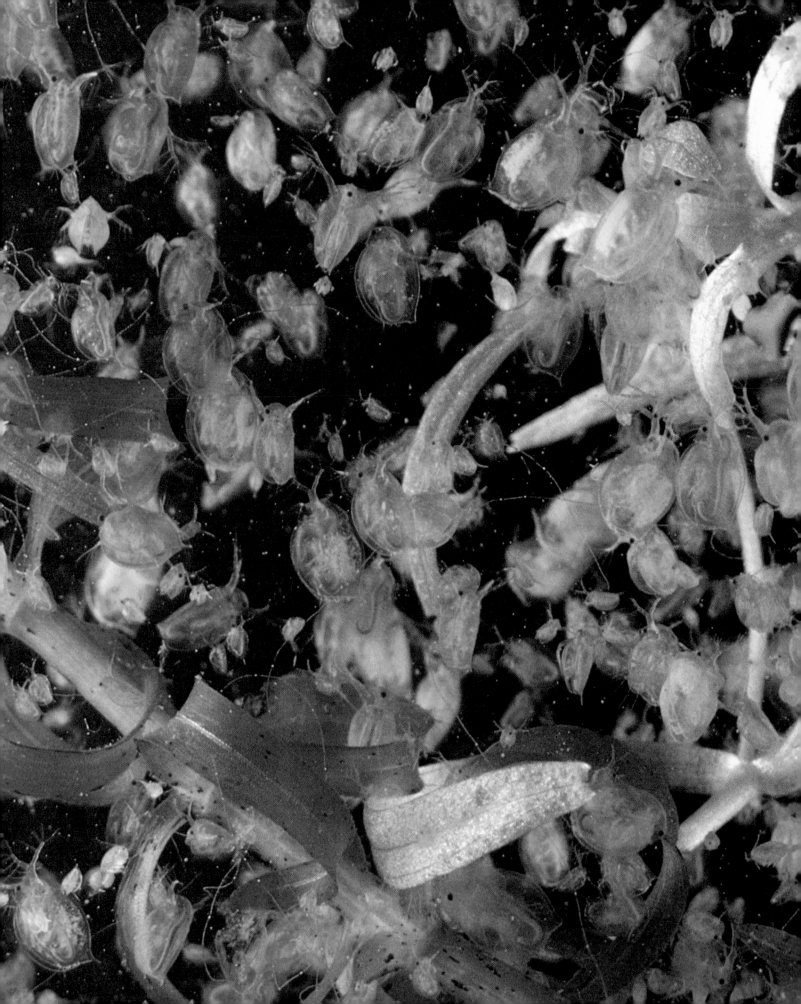

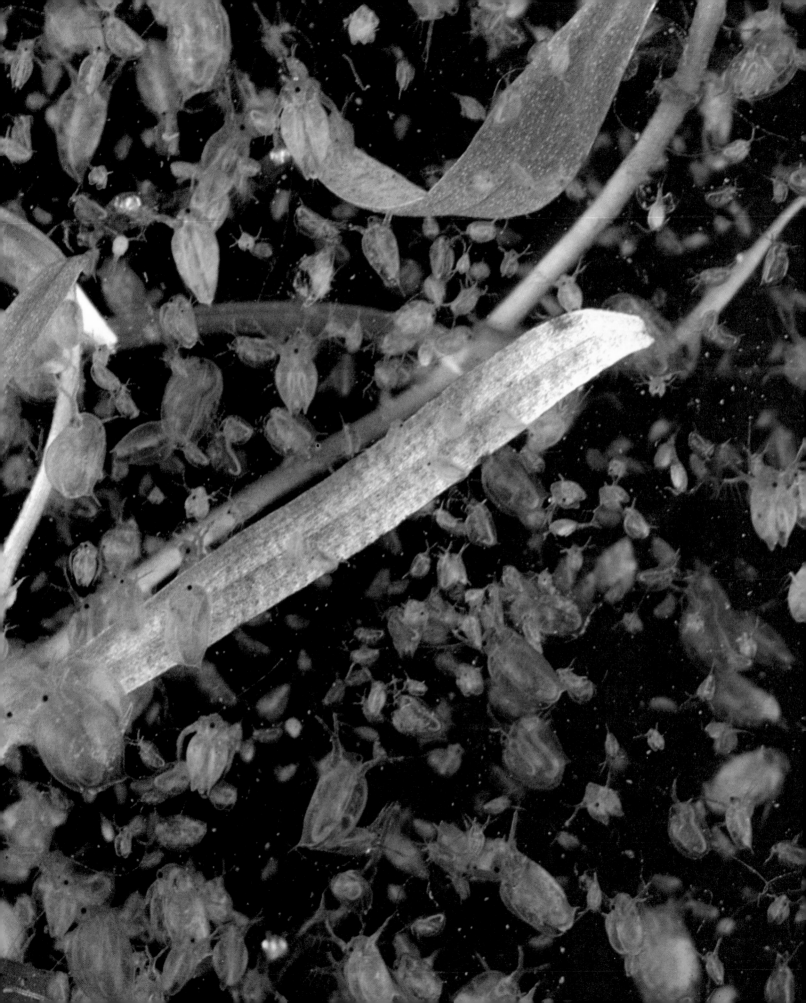

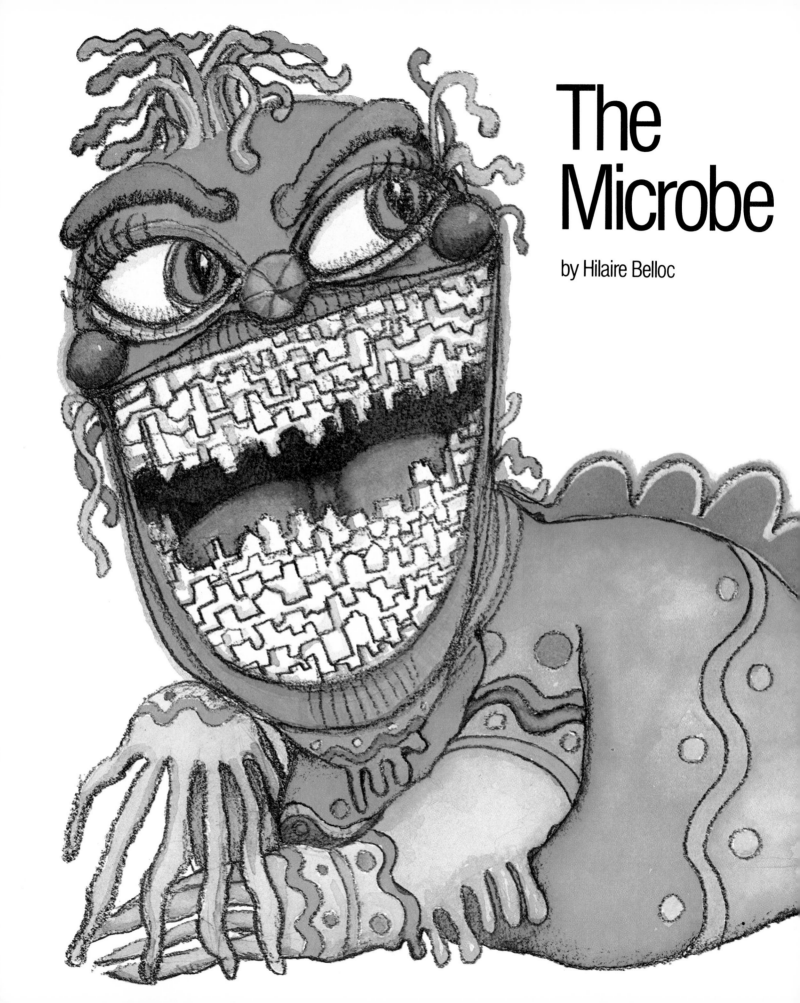

The Microbe

by Hilaire Belloc

Born in France, Hilaire Belloc adopted England as his home and was successful as an essayist, historian and poet. In popular collections of poetry such as Cautionary Verses, *which contributes the poem reprinted here, Belloc sees with a child's eye.*

The Microbe is so very small
You cannot make him out at all,
But many sanguine people hope
To see him through a microscope.
His jointed tongue that lies beneath
A hundred curious rows of teeth;
His seven tufted tails with lots
Of lovely pink and purple spots,
On each of which a pattern stands,
Composed of forty separate bands;
His eyebrows of a tender green;
All these have never yet been seen—
But Scientists, who ought to know,
Assure us that they must be so....
Oh! let us never, never doubt
What nobody is sure about!

Jelly Stingers

Even among the almost innumerable variety of life-forms in the sea, the coelenterates, a group that includes such spineless creatures as jellyfish, corals, sea anemones and hydroids, are so enormously diverse that they seem to belie their kinship with one another. The diaphanous, pulsating jellyfish range from rare Arctic creatures that measure seven feet in diameter through more familiar saucer- and coin-sized versions to a great number of pinheads that are all but invisible to the naked eye. In contrast to these free-floating forms are the corals, stationary bottom dwellers whose stony skeletons have piled up to form the great reefs. Similar in their sessile life-style are the sea anemones, which wave like flowers in underwater gardens. Hydrozoans are strange animals that look like moss or tiny ferns carpeting the sea floor. Hydrozoans often form colonies; some stand on the bottom, resembling foot-high reeds, and others, like the Portuguese man-of-war, sail the open seas.

Beneath their diverse exteriors, however, all of these creatures share a single master plan. As the name of the group suggests (Coelenterata means "hollow gut"), each of these creatures is little more than a sack with a single opening that is surrounded by one or more rings of tentacles. In their commonest form, coelenterates have only two layers of cells—one lining the inside of the sack and the other covering the outside. Sandwiched between them, giving support and shape, is a gelatinous substance that gives jellyfish their name.

Life functions in the more than 9,000 species of coelenterates are as simply organized as is their anatomy. The inner wall of cells, which produces digestive juices as well as eggs or sperm, takes care of the bodily processes of digestion and reproduction. The coelenterate's body, by means of expansions and contractions, draws in food and expels waste along with eggs or sperm. The outer wall of cells provides protection and stuns prey by means of thousands of stinging cells, called nematocysts, that are concentrated mostly in the tentacles.

There are really only two basic variations on the sack design. One is a free-floating, umbrella- or bell-shaped form typical of jellyfish. Called medusae, such animals drift with their mouths turned downward and their fringe of tentacles dangling into the plankton-rich waters below. The other variation on this configuration is the polyp, which is almost the inverse of the medusa. Usually permanently anchored to the seabed, a polyp has a tubular stalklike shape with a mouth at the top, surrounded by a circle of tentacles extending upward and outward like delicate branches. In a seesaw process known as alternation of generations, common among many coelenterates, parents and their offspring shift back and forth, by turns, between the two forms. Jellyfish, for example, spend only one generation as floating medusae. Their fertilized eggs, after only a brief larval stage spent nestled in the parent's tentacles, sink to the ocean floor and grow into polyps. In turn, these polyps produce young that drift off and develop into gossamer floating mushrooms—medusae just like their grandparents.

Much the same thing happens among many species of hydrozoans in which the polyp stage is dominant (corresponding to the medusa stage in scyphozoan, or true, jellyfish). However, in one group of hydrozoans called siphonophores, polyps and medusae join together in drifting colonies. Most of these individuals have specialized functions corresponding to those of organs, and the colony is usually although erroneously thought of as a single animal. The best-known siphonophore is that formidable dreadnought, the Portuguese man-of-war. An extremely common sight in almost every sea and ocean, this curious "creature" is really a colony of polyps hanging from a gas-filled translucent float. Ranging in length from six to 12 inches, the float not only looks like a sail but actually functions as one. Beneath it, hundreds of polyps form a net of deadly tentacles that may extend some 60 feet below the surface. Some of these members handle digestion, others reproduction, while still others specialize in stinging prey.

Another group of gelatinous drifters, the delicately beautiful comb jellies in some ways resemble the siphonophores and jellyfish, but represent a phylum of their own: Ctenophora. Anatomically, they are very different from the coelenterates; they use the comblike rows of filaments from which they take their name like the oars of a racing shell to propel themselves through the water. More notably, they do not have stinging cells.

Although they lack this lethal armament, comb jellies are among the sea's more voracious creatures. One sea gooseberry, a globe about an inch in diameter that has two tentacles nearly two feet long lined with sticky threads, which drag the water like flypaper, was discovered with five herring fry in its stomach.

Each tentacle of the Portuguese man-of-war (left) is a specially modified polyp. The flask-shaped ones are in charge of digestion. The coiled tentacles are lined with nematocysts for defense, while the polyps that look like strings of beads are the sensory members of the colony.

The gas-filled float of a Portuguese man-of-war bobs along the surface of the ocean (below). The crest across its top catches the wind like a sail to help propel the entire colony through the water.

Deadly Streamers

The most complex and fascinating of all coelenterates are the siphonophores—beautiful floating colonies composed of several different kinds of individuals, some medusa-like, some polyp-like, all joined to form a single, functioning cooperative. Each individual is specialized so that it can perform a particular function within the complex: either reproduction, digestion, defense or locomotion. The Portuguese man-of-war, *Physalia physalis*, is without doubt the best-known of the siphonophores, and gatherings of thousands of them are a familiar sight in tropical seas. The man-of-war's iridescent float, or pneumatophore, which is often tinged with pink or orange, is responsible for the locomotion of the entire group. Filled with gas, the float sits passively on the water's surface until nudged by the wind, when it can skim across the water at speeds of up to 65 feet per minute. Carried along beneath the float is a tangle of tentacles each of which is lined with numerous nematocysts, or stinging cells, arranged in knobby clusters. These cells pack a potent poison capable of paralyzing fish as large as the man-of-war itself. Human beings are also vulnerable to the man-of-war's sting, which causes intense burning and irritation.

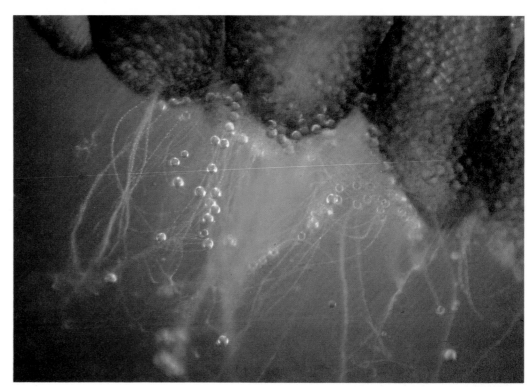

Under magnification, a Portuguese man-of-war's nematocysts (above) "fire" deadly thread tubes, the actual stinging agents. These tiny hairlike harpoons are hollow and contain a paralyzing poison. Each thread tube can be used only once; after it has been fired, the entire nematocyst is digested along with the food it has helped to catch.

The tentacles of a Portuguese man-of-war dangle in the water, suspended from the colony's float (left). These tentacles are often as long as 60 feet. As the man-of-war drifts along, they trail behind like a net—trapping any particle of food with which they come in contact.

A tiny parasitic flatworm, colored brown in the picture at right, nestles undisturbed in a coiled defense tentacle of a Portuguese man-of-war. Although these tentacles are lined with stinging nematocysts, the flatworm fails to trigger the cells' stinging apparatus.

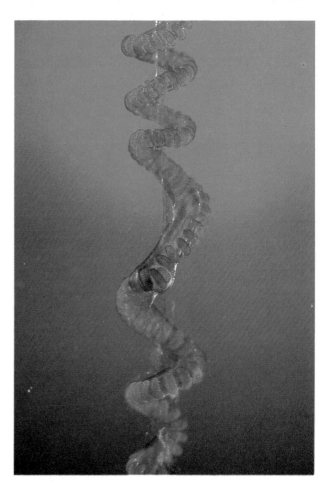

Paralyzed by the tentacles of a Portuguese man-of-war, a fish is slowly digested by special feeding polyps called gastrozooids. As particles of the victim are broken down by the digestive juices secreted by the gastrozooids, the food is absorbed and distributed to all the members of the colony through a common gastrovascular system.

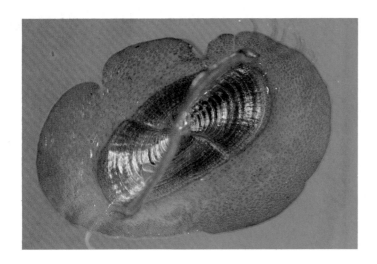

Viewed from the top (above) and side (above, right), a velella sets sail and cruises. Its float is an oblong about two and a half inches long, with the sail set diagonally across the top.

In side and top views (below and at right), a porpita extends its tentacles in order to catch food. These sailless siphonophores are abundant in the waters around Florida.

A Handy Sailor

Siphonophores—primarily tropical and semitropical animals—come in various shapes and sizes and in colors that echo the hues of the ocean, ranging from sea green to deep purple or blue. Siphonophores are generally larger than hydrozoan jellyfish, and some have the ability to regulate the gas content of their floats. When the weather is pleasant, the float fills up with gas and catches the wind at the ocean's surface. During violent ocean storms, however, some species of siphonophores are able to deflate their floats, which lets the entire colony sink beneath the water's surface, safe from the force of the crashing waves above.

Two of the commonest siphonophores are *Velella* and its cousin, *Porpita*, which has a flattened disklike float. *Velella* has earned the name Jack-sail-by-the-wind because it tacks like a sailboat carried by wind and water currents. *Velella* can also control its movement by means of its tentacles, which have fibers capable of contracting and expanding. By expanding and stretching out its tentacles as far as possible to create a drag, a velella can prevent a strong wind from driving it ashore.

Generation Gaps

Most hydrozoans reproduce through an alternation of generations. In this process a polyp asexually buds a medusa, and then the medusa produces gametes—eggs and sperm—that unite to form a larva, which will develop into a polyp just like its grandparent. But different hydrozoans play different variations on this reproductive theme. *Tubularia*, for example, does not produce free-swimming medusae. The medusae instead remain attached to their parent polyp and are so specialized that all they do is generate gametes, which unite to produce a stocky hydra-like larva, called an actinula, that can creep across the ocean floor on its tentacles or float in the plankton. In *Pennaria*, free-swimming medusae are budded from polyps, gametes are released, and a swimming larva, or planula, is formed. After a while both actinula and planula settle on a surface and produce new polyp colonies. In yet another variation, *Gonionemus* can sometimes skip the asexual phase altogether. Its medusae produce planulae that are capable of developing through an actinular stage into new medusae —without ever becoming polyps.

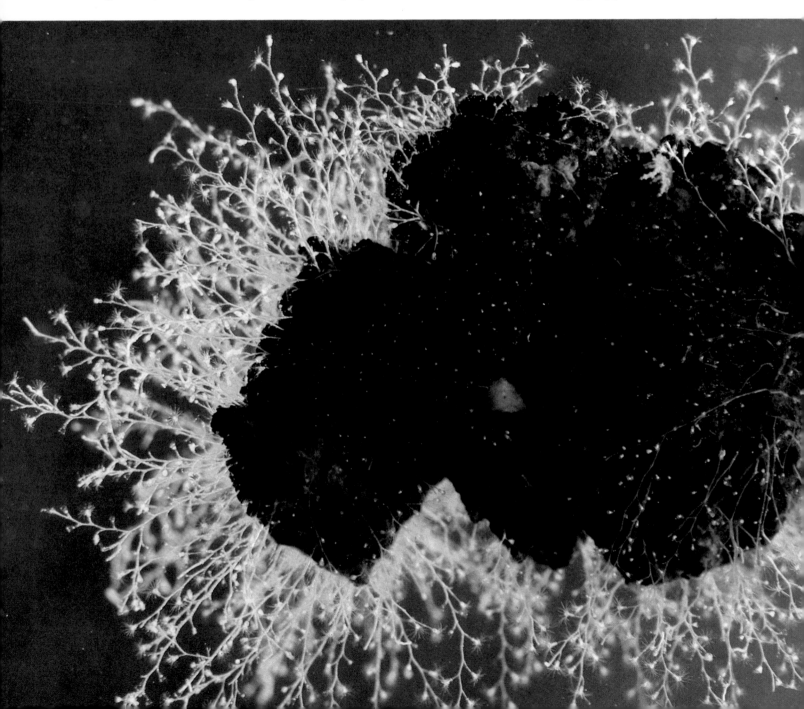

Attached to a lump of crude oil (below), a colony of hydroids floats in the ocean. Such groups of hydrozoan polyps are usually sessile—they live attached to surfaces such as rocks, shells or wharf pilings—and are often mistaken for seaweed. Tubularia colonies are especially adaptable, and have even been found inside live sponges.

Fully extended, the delicate tentacles of Pennaria polyps (above) give the entire colony a fernlike appearance. Hydrozoan colonies are found mostly in coastal waters, and are usually an eighth of an inch to eight inches long. But one species has been known to produce colonies that stretch seven feet or more, and other colonies have been found at a depth of as much as 500 fathoms (3,000 feet).

Tubularia produces an exact miniature duplicate of itself, which remains attached to its parent and eventually generates its own offspring.

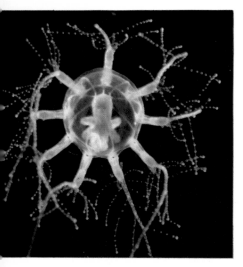

The Cladonema medusa lives free until it releases eggs and sperm.

A hydromedusa moves by opening and shutting its umbrella.

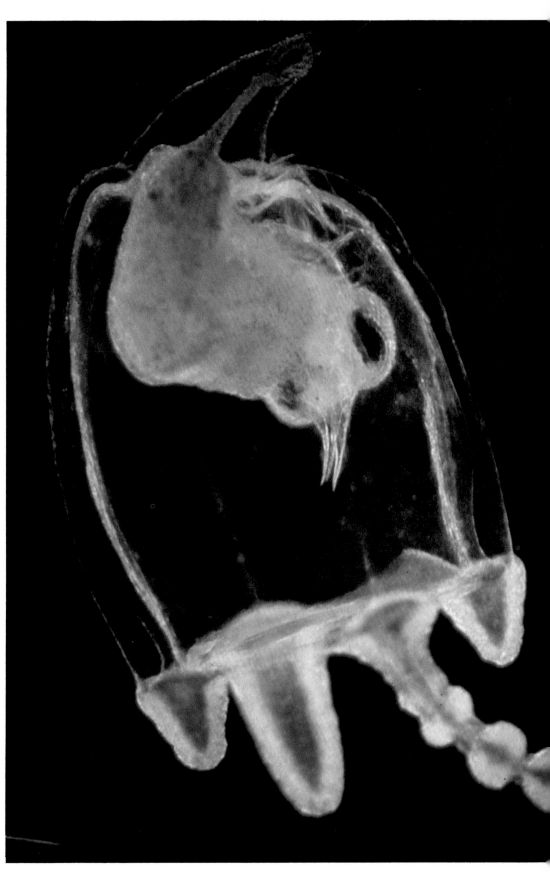

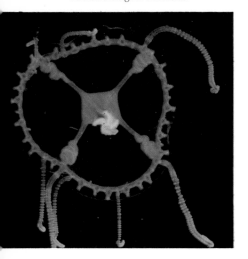

The clumps on this Gonionemus medusa are gonads.

A decapod larva is digested by a hydromedusa (left). Hydrozoans feed on anything they can find, and can ingest crustaceans and larvae their own size.

A hydromedusa fishes for planktonic prey by jet-propelling itself to the ocean's surface and then floating down with its tentacles outstretched.

Polyps of Aurelia attach themselves to the ocean bottom (left). When mature, each polyp will produce larvae called ephyrae that form on it like a stack of disks. Ephyrae are produced every year for several years, and take about five months to reach a sexually mature form like that of Periphylla (below).

A mature Haliclystus, firmly attached to seaweed, extends its tentacles in starbursts (right). Haliclystus is one of the rare stalked scyphozoan jellies, a small species whose umbrella is only one inch in diameter.

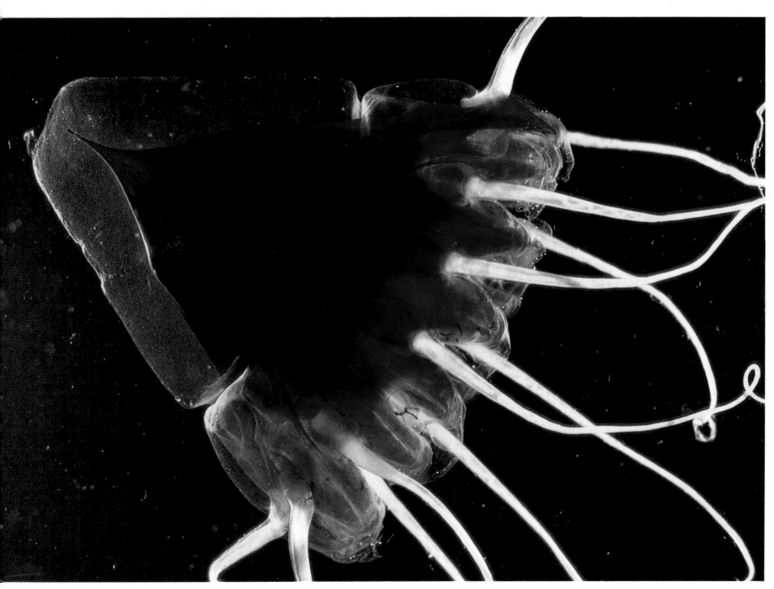

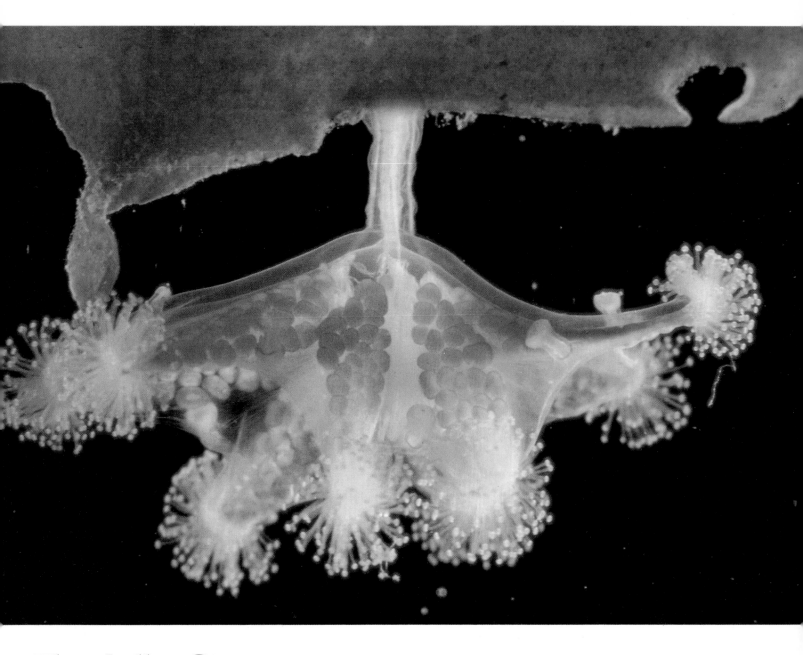

The Jelly Giants

Though most scyphozoan jellyfish are, like the hydrozoans, fairly small, the group boasts a wide range of sizes. Many species, such as *Haliclystus*, are button sized, but *Cyanea capillata*, an inhabitant of Arctic waters, grows as large as seven feet in diameter and has tentacles more than 100 feet long. Some scyphozoan jellyfish feed by jet-propelling themselves to the surface of the water and floating down with their umbrellas open to catch their prey. The surface of the umbrella is covered with ciliated bands of sticky mucus, and the edges of the mouth are extended into four "oral arms." Plankton is trapped in the mucus, swept by the cilia toward the rim of the umbrella, and then licked off by the oral arms and carried into the mouth for ingestion. Other scyphozoan jellyfish catch their food with their tentacles and oral arms.

The oral arms also play a role in reproduction. Gametes of the scyphozoan jellyfish are deposited in the gastrovascular cavity rather than directly in the water. They lodge and unite in the frills of the oral arms and are brooded there before being set free as swimming larvae.

Stick-to-Itiveness

The casual observer might lump the comb jellies, or ctenophores, with cnidarian jellyfish such as the scyphozoan
and hydrozoan jellyfish, but though both are blobs of jelly
with tentacles, the two are quite different. Rather than moving by pulsation, comb jellies move by rapidly beating
plates composed of cilia, arranged in eight vertical rows,
that look a little like the teeth of a comb. While cnidarian
jellyfish usually have many tentacles, comb jellies have
only two. These tentacles, located on opposite sides of the
comb jelly's body, extend from two deep pouches into
which they can rapidly retract. Each tentacle is equipped
with adhesive cells called colloblasts, which secrete a
sticky substance when touched. Once a creature is stuck to
the colloblast there is usually no escape. Some ctenophores
are able to consume fish twice their size, and a fleet of comb
jellies can clear an area of young fish and the crustaceans
they feed on—a fact that has not endeared them to com-
mercial fishermen.

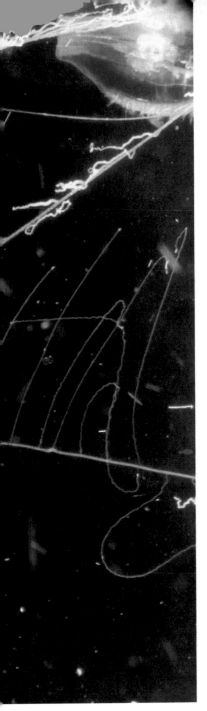

Two Pleurobrachia *comb jellies,
or sea gooseberries, move
through the ocean with their
tentacles trailing (left). Comb
jellies are usually propelled
mouth forward by undulations
of the rows of ciliary combs
along their sides, but they can
also reverse direction to make a
hasty retreat from danger.*

During the day, the ciliated
bands of the comb jelly
Mnemiopsis *glow colorfully
(right). At night, they are
phosphorescent.* Mnemiopsis *is
a lobate ctenophore—a group
whose flattened bodies and
constricted midsections result in
two lobes at the mouth end—
giving them a clamlike shape.*

A hydrozoan jellyfish,
Aequorea, *on top in the picture
at right, and a comb jelly,*
Mnemiopsis, *do battle. Though
of comparable size,*
Mnemiopsis' *usually effective
sticky tentacles are no match for
the stinging cells on the
tentacles of* Aequorea, *and the
jellyfish can capture and eat the
comb jelly with little difficulty.*

Under the Sea Wind

by Rachel Carson

Marine biologist Rachel Carson pioneered in exposing man's abuse of the natural world. She has also been acclaimed for her poetic descriptions of life in the sea. In the following passage from Under the Sea Wind *she captures the drama of a young mackerel's encounter with a comb jelly.*

As Scomber pursued the larvae in emerald haze five fathoms under the surface he saw a bright flash sweep in a blinding arc across his sphere of vision. Almost instantly the flash was followed by a second blaze of iridescent glitter that curved sharply upward and seemed to thicken as it moved toward a shimmering oval globe above. Once more the thread of the tentacle crept down, all its cilia ablaze in the sunlight. Scomber's instincts warned him of danger, although never before in his larval life had he encountered one of the race of Pleurobrachia, the comb jelly, the foe of all young fishes.

Of a sudden, like a rope swiftly uncoiling from a hand above, one of the tentacles was dropped more than two feet below the inch-long body of the ctenophore, and thus swiftly extended it looped around the tail of Scomber. The tentacle was set with a lateral row of hairlike threads, as barbs grow from the shaft of a bird's feather, but the threads were filmy and tenuous as the strands of a spider's web. All the lateral hairs of the tentacle poured out a gluelike secretion, causing Scomber to become hopelessly entangled in the many threads. He strove to escape, beating the water with his fins and flexing his body violently. The tentacle, contracting and enlarging steadily from the

thickness of a hair to that of a thread and then to that of a fishing line, drew him closer and closer to the mouth of the comb jelly. Now he was within an inch of the cold, smooth-surfaced blob of jelly that spun gently in the water. The creature, like a gooseberry in shape, lay in the water with the mouth uppermost, keeping its position by an easy, monotonous beating of the eight rows of ciliated plates or combs. The sun that found its way down from above set the cilia aglow with a radiance that half blinded Scomber as he was drawn up along the slippery body of his foe.

In another instant he would have been seized by the lobelike lips of the creature's mouth and passed into the central sac of its body, there to be digested; but for the moment he was saved by the fact that the ctenophore had caught him while it was still in the midst of digesting another meal. From its mouth there protruded the tail and hinder third of a young herring it had caught half an hour before. The comb jelly was greatly distended, for the herring was much too large to be swallowed whole. Although it had tried by violent contractions to force all of the her-ring past its lips it was unable to do so and had perforce to wait until enough of the fish was digested to make room for the tail. Scomber was held in further reserve, to be eaten after the herring.

In spite of his spasmodic struggles, Scomber was unable to break away from the entangling net of the tentacle hairs, and moment by moment his efforts grew feebler. Steadily and inexorably the contortions of the comb jelly's body were drawing the herring farther into the deadly sac, where digestive ferments worked with marvelous speed to con-vert the fish tissues, by subtle alchemy, into food for the ctenophore.

Now a dark shadow came between Scomber and the sun. A great, torpedo-shaped body loomed in the water and a cavernous mouth opened and engulfed the ctenophore, the herring, and the entrapped mackerel. A two-year-old sea trout mouthed the watery body of the comb jelly, crushed it experimentally against the roof of its mouth, and spat it out in disgust. With it went Scomber, half dead with pain and exhaustion, but freed from the grip of the dead ctenophore.

Mollusks

Commonly restricted to land or to the bottom of the sea by the weight of their shells, gastropods such as snails, limpets and whelks might appear to be the least likely animals to have close kin with a means for getting around in the open sea. Yet numbers of tiny mollusks are to be found as members of the sea's plankton. Living in many levels of the ocean, they may well be as abundant as their fellow land gastropods are. And like many other denizens of the sea, most have made unusual adaptations that enable them to survive and move about.

The most numerous group of sea snails, the pteropods, which are usually a half inch in size or smaller, often have spiraling shells that are delicate miniatures of the shells of their terrestrial relatives. In place of the single large muscular foot characteristic of most mollusks, the pteropod has a foot with two winglike flaps that the animal uses to paddle through the water. The scientific name Pteropoda means "wing footed," and these appendages have also inspired the popular name sea butterfly. In motion, however, a pteropod bears little resemblance to a dainty butterfly. Taking an indirect and often reeling course, most pteropods careen through the sea by flailing their wings; some species flap so vigorously that their bodies bounce up and down.

Even the larvae of pteropods, and of other sea snails as well, must work hard to stay afloat. Called veligers, the larvae begin their lives equipped with a shell; in order to maintain their weight in the water without sinking, they must keep their ciliated lobes, often of extreme length in proportion to the size of their bodies, constantly and energetically in motion.

Despite their lack of grace in motion, pteropods include some of the ocean's most beautiful inhabitants. Although some, with sepia shells and charcoal bodies, look like winged versions of their land-snail relatives, others have much more streamlined shells that resemble tiny cones, boats and pointed shoes. In some pteropods, like Clio, the shell resembles tinted glass and the wings are subtly colored. In others, like Cymbulia, which is also aptly known as Venus' slipper, a delicate crystalline transparency in both shell and body makes detection extremely difficult even in a laboratory dish. These pteropods are so numerous that in death they layer many tropical seabeds with thick deposits of their shells, a decomposing muck commonly referred to as pteropod ooze. Alongside the shelled pteropods are those that brave the ocean with little or no comparable protection. Prominent among them is the shell-less Clione, which makes up for its ethereal appearance, conferred by a diaphanous body and fluttering wings, by preying voraciously on its fellow pteropods.

An even stranger group of seafearing snails is the heteropods—which must rank as top contenders for the title of the world's oddest-looking creatures. A typical heteropod has a thin, fragile shell, so small that it has room only for a heart and gills. The rest of its body, which is transparent and sometimes tinged with pale ocher, has become flattened and elongated and has developed a finlike wing. It would look like a fanciful fish—except for the trunk protruding from its front like an elephant's. The heteropod, slightly more nimble than the pteropod, swims upside down, using its tiny shell as a keel. Rolling and twisting from side to side as it flaps its single wing back and forth like a sculling oar, it can propel itself through the water at a fairly brisk pace.

Although some heteropods have shells and others have none, all of them are variations of the same outlandish model. Relatively large for members of the plankton, they range in size from under an inch to nearly a foot. Most of them are gluttonous predators, and they are capable of catching formidable prey: One heteropod was found with the remains of six fish inside it, all of them nearly as long as their captor.

Neither a pteropod nor a heteropod, another sea snail has evolved a remarkable sort of drifter's life in the sea. One of the few pelagic animals that live permanently on the surface, the beautiful deep violet Janthina hangs upside down from a self-made raft of bubbles. This creature, which looks much like an ordinary snail, constructs its raft by trapping air bubbles with its slimy foot, which then coats the bubbles with mucus. As the bubbles harden, more are added, and the result is a tough, clear multichambered air mattress that is hard to puncture, with more than enough buoyancy to support its passenger.

Janthina sometimes becomes a victim of its own drifting way of life. Often traveling in large flotillas, the snails, unable to sink beneath the surface, can be caught by a gale and tossed onto the shore, where they are completely helpless. The fragile shells are soon crushed by the storm-driven surf. The result, sometimes seen on Florida beaches after a harsh easterly, is a purple band that stretches for miles at the high-tide line.

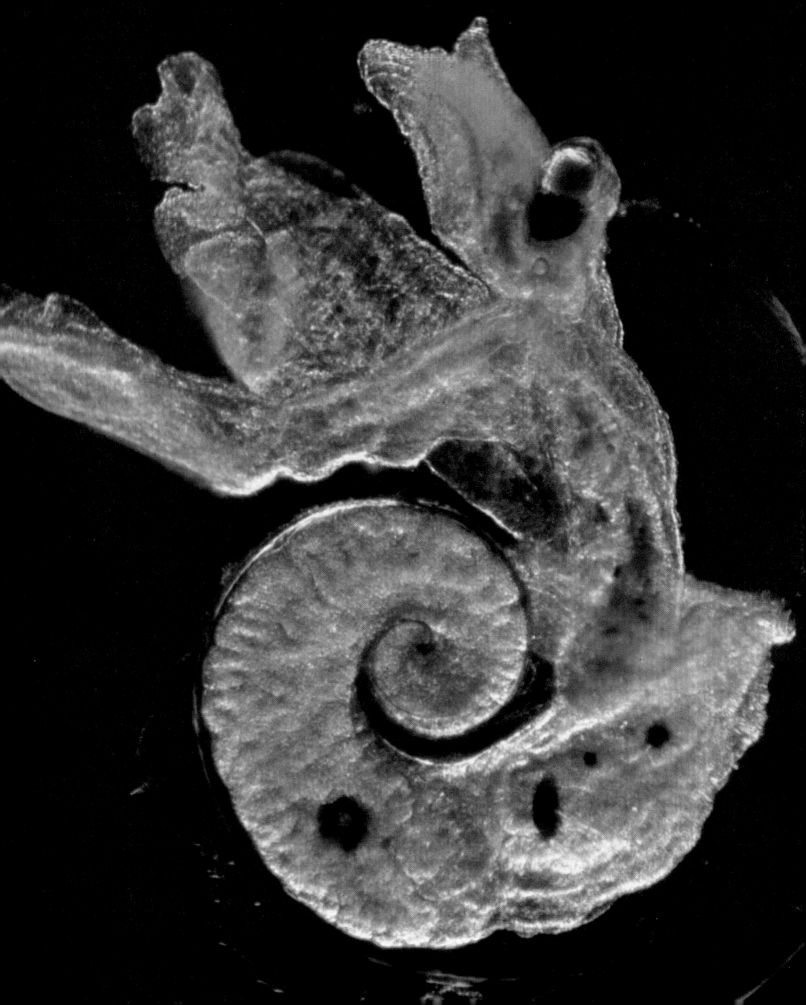

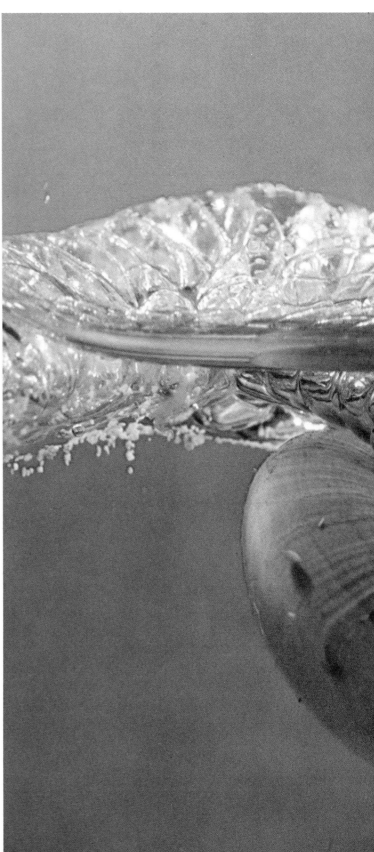

Egg cases (left) may be deposited by a female *Janthina* in clutches of up to 500 with up to two and a half million eggs. Ten to 12 days after the eggs are laid they burst open to release swimming larvae.

Snails at the Surface

Many sea snails are bottom dwellers, specifically adapted to live on the sea floor. But although it is a shelled gastropod like some of its bottom-dwelling sea-snail relatives, the pelagic *Janthina* has special modifications for life on the ocean's surface. The delicate shell is lightweight and more fragile than that of the bottom dwellers, so *Janthina* is easily suspended from the bubble raft-float that it builds for itself. Its foot, which has adapted beyond its function as an organ of locomotion, has a specialized gland that produces a clear, resilient material. Bubbles of this substance harden into the sturdy raft, and *Janthina* drifts along, hanging upside down from the raft's underside. Encapsulated eggs are deposited beneath the raft, transforming it into a floating incubator for larvae.

When *Janthina's* raft collides with the siphonophore *Velella*, the snail exudes a violet liquid that apparently anesthetizes *Velella*. *Janthina* then has a leisurely meal, nibbling away on its victim, including the poisonous tentacles—to which it seems immune—until all that remains is *Velella's* own sailboat-like raft.

Having immobilized Velella, or "Jack-sail-by-the-wind" jellyfish (below), Janthina proceeds to cut off chunks of its victim's body, using its raspy "tongue," or radula.

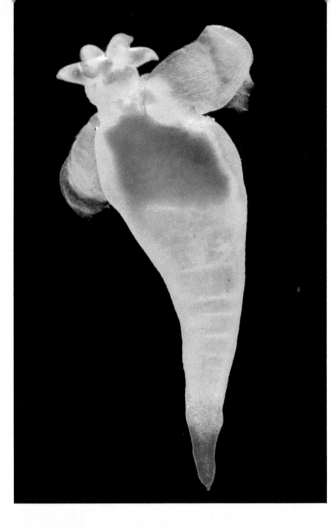

Wings gently flapping, Clione charts an oscillating course through the ocean depths. Vulnerable because of its lack of a shell, it is nevertheless a voracious predator, often victimizing fellow pteropods.

A transparent, swirled shell coils protectively around a limacinid pteropod's soft body (below). This sea butterfly's wings flutter and droop gracefully, like those of its airborne namesake.

A cavolinid pteropod (below) descends in the water and extends its wings to slow its downward progress. These appendages are also feeding mechanisms: Their movement directs food toward the pteropod's mouth.

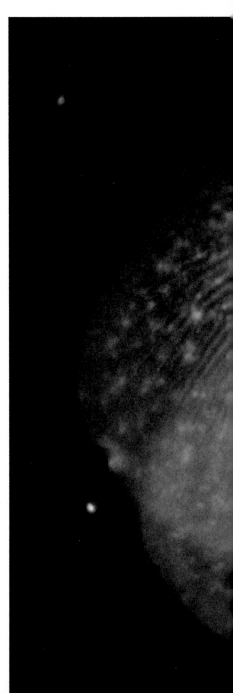

Vertical Commuters

In the mollusks called pteropods, or sea butterflies, the gastropod foot has developed into a divided appendage resembling a pair of wings that is the means of locomotion for these free-swimming marine snails. By agitating this organ, the pteropod can propel itself up or down in a spiraling motion.

Often pteropods, like other planktonic organisms, will wing along in one ocean current by day and then migrate vertically to locate in another current, usually nearer the surface, at night. Although their progress is jerky and intermittent, it is surprisingly effective. Some pteropods, such as *Clione*, have no shells; others, like *Cavolinia*, can retract into their armor at the least sign of danger.

The heteropods shown overleaf are also swimming sea snails but belong to a different group of gastropods. In the heteropods the snail foot takes the form of a single fin that acts as an oar, propelling the animal erratically but vigorously forward.

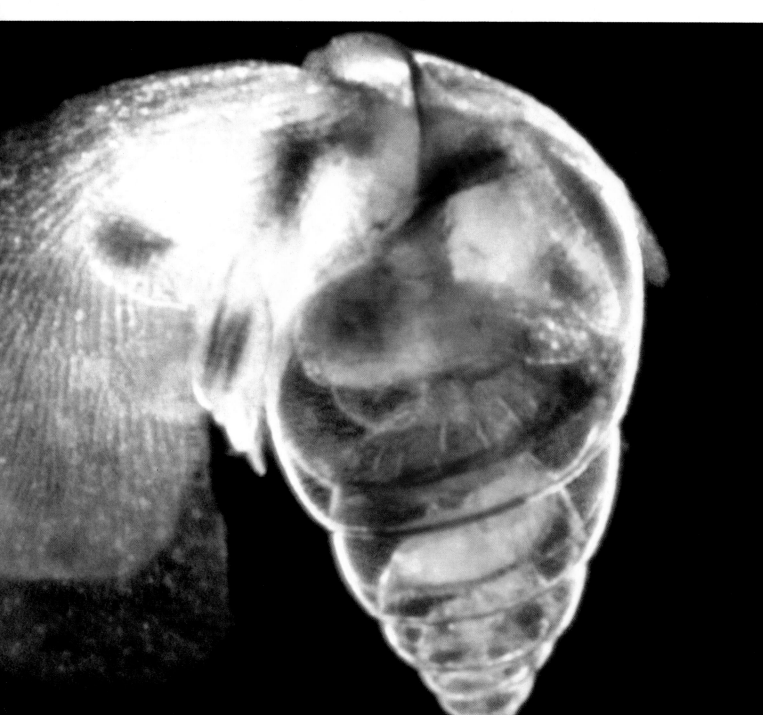

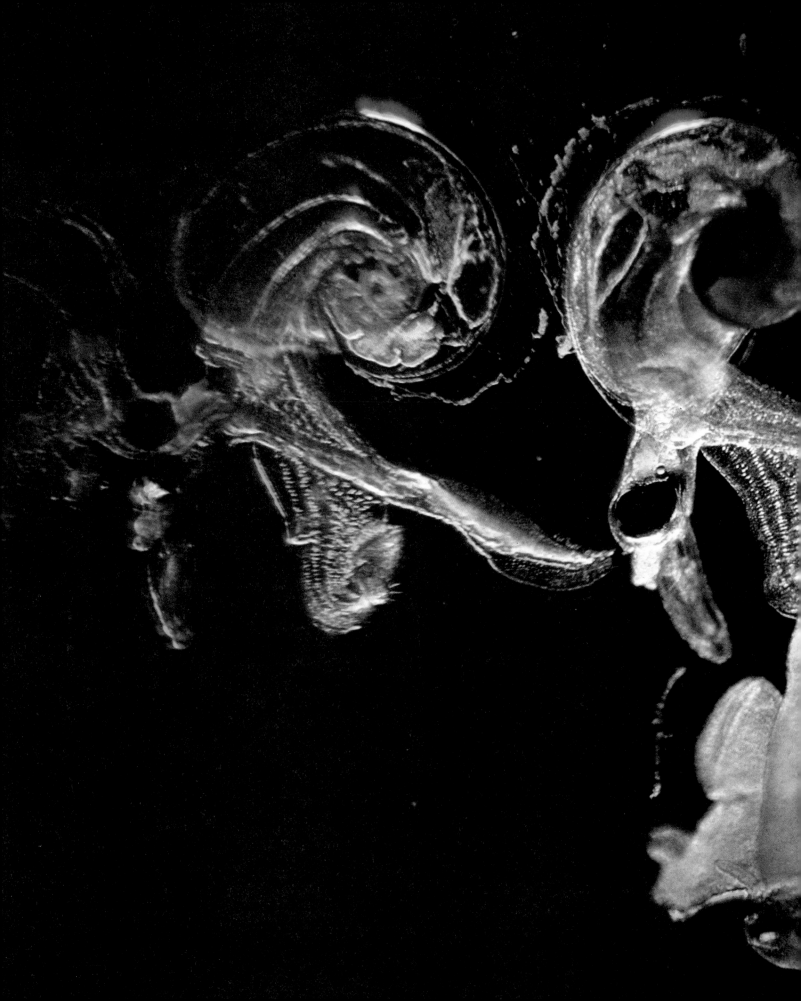

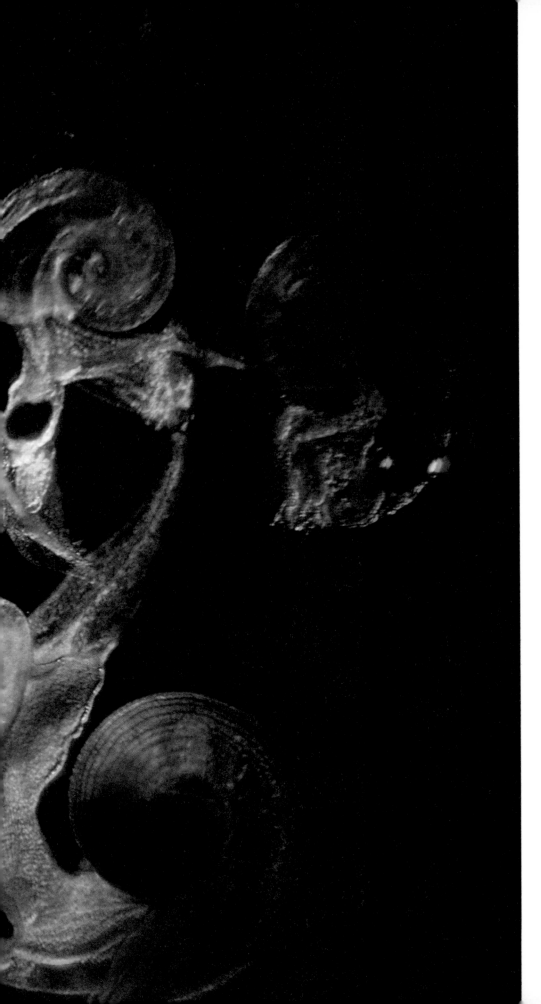

A heteropod suspends
itself, using its shell as ballast,
and maneuvers with its finlike
foot. Some heteropods attain a
body length of 10 inches and are
highly predacious, attacking
and ingesting almost any
animal they can overcome.

Advanced Invertebrates

As a buoyant and hospitable environment for animals without backbones, the ocean's waters have afforded a splendid arena for their evolution, not least for those that are members of the oceanic plankton. In this company, the larvae of fish contain the visible but incompleted matrices of spines, but others, such as the cylindrical salps, either lack a skeleton altogether or, like the crustaceans, wear it on the outside. With their exoskeletons, hearts, gills and eyes, and sensitive antennae, the crustaceans are the most successful of the sea's advanced invertebrates, and they have assumed a status equal to that occupied on land by their uncountable relatives, the insects.

While the word crustacean usually brings to mind only the larger members of this group—the lobsters, crabs, shrimps, prawns and crayfish that occasionally grace the dinner table—the oceans of the world are almost literally crawling with their lesser-known kin. Many are close cousins of these familiar shellfish. Some, such as the blind, spidery-legged crab *Ethusa*, are seldom glimpsed because they scurry about in the depths of the oceans. Others are rarely seen because they are scaled-down versions of their larger relatives; examples are the tiny, aptly named pea crabs, which live in the mantle cavity of clams, and euphausids, the shrimplike krill that furnish the diet of the giant humpback and blue whales, which gulp them down by the millions.

The most numerous of these diminutive creatures are probably the copepods. About the size of pinheads, copepods are not only the commonest crustaceans but also the most abundant multicellular animals in the sea. Indeed, they may outnumber all the world's other animals combined. During the spring bloom, when the sea becomes a lush meadow filled with microscopic plants, the minute, mostly vegetarian copepods multiply with a rapidity that would boggle a computer. Thousands occupy a cubic yard of water; in one study, a quarter hour of trawling yielded an estimated two and a half million copepods.

Taken from a tow net and observed under a microscope, copepods, diversified into more than 4,000 known species, are bizarrely beautiful. Many resemble brightly tinted spun-glass shrimp. They usually have six pairs of feathery legs, which in some species flutter 600 times a minute to keep the animals from sinking. Their legs bristle with a profusion of whisker-like plumes for straining their food from the planktonic soup. The most striking aspects of many copepods' appearance is a single eye in the center of the head. This Cyclopean feature is not a handicap: The eye is composed of three useful ocular units—one looking downward and two scanning upward and forward.

Although not as plentiful as the copepods, the ocean's other tiny crustaceans are nonetheless numerous—and often even stranger in appearance: for example, the ostracods. The largest is the deepwater dweller *Gigantocypris*, which, despite its name, measures a mere half inch across. *Gigantocypris* has a see-through bivalved shell and looks like a deep-orange miniature mussel that has sprouted plumelike legs; its enormous eyes resemble automobile headlights. Apparently more complicated than the ostracods are such crustaceans as the flealike amphipods and the isopods, licelike animals some of which follow a parasitic life-style, frequently attaching themselves to crustaceans, fish and other animals. The peculiar goose barnacle, hidden inside an opaque shell, also lives in a state of permanent attachment to something else, usually the undersides of drifting objects—bottles, planks, sargassum weed and even viscous oil slicks.

In addition to the crustaceans, a sample of zooplankton often yields a mass of floating fish eggs. Carried aimlessly on the surface currents, they will hatch into helpless larvae. And patrolling the rich waters in search of a meal, the swiftly darting arrowworms, second only to the copepods in number, aggressively prey on the fish larvae as well as on other zooplankton. When one of these three-quarter-inch transparent carnivorous creatures gobbles a herring fry, the result looks like a plastic-wrapped fish from the market—dollhouse sized.

Fish larvae, as the plankton's only vertebrates, are its most sophisticated representatives in an evolutionary sense. Just below them on the evolutionary scale are the salps, pelagic relatives of the coastal-dwelling sea squirts. Salps and sea squirts, called tunicates or urochordates, are among the most advanced invertebrates in the sea, and are ancestral to the vertebrates. Their larvae possess a notochord—a forerunner of the backbone—and a dorsal nerve cord and gill slits. Shooting through the water using a form of jet propulsion, salps, which look like tiny crystalline barrels, are preyed upon by one ingenious crustacean. After eating the inside of a salp, the amphipod *Phronima* stashes her young in the hollowed-out chamber and rolls them along as if they were in a seagoing baby carriage.

Copepod

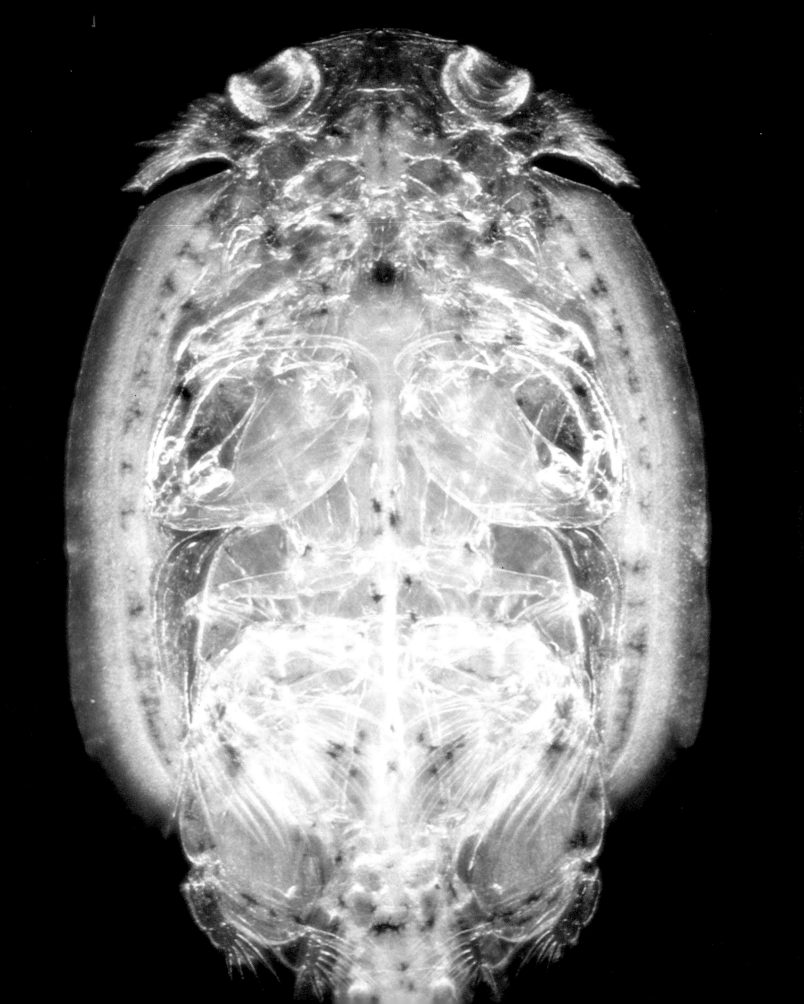

Swarming Copepods

Swirling about in their briny universe, the animals called copepods feed and reproduce on a massive scale that belies their minuscule size. Although individual organisms rarely exceed two thirds of an inch in length, they have a substantial cumulative effect on the marine ecosystem. Many of them function like tiny protein-conversion machines, turning phytoplankton, or plant matter, into the protein-rich tissue of their own bodies, on which enormous numbers of other ocean creatures feed. When the random orbit of a herbivorous copepod crosses that of a phytoplankter, the copepod's anterior limbs scoop up and strain the plant matter out of the water. The limbs are fringed with setae—tiny filaments that perform the filtering process. Some copepod species are carnivorous, seizing zooplankton prey with their anterior limbs, squeezing it between their mandibles and devouring it voraciously. Others, such as *Caligus*, parasitize fish, clinging to their skin and sucking their blood.

Copepods are prolific, reproducing by sexual means: The male delivers sperm in its funnel-shaped spermatophore to the female. A female may be approached by two or more males, and mating may take up to 30 minutes.

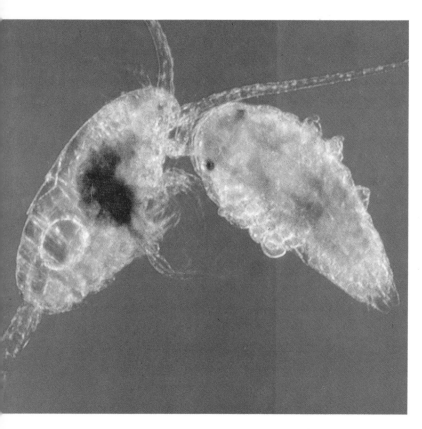

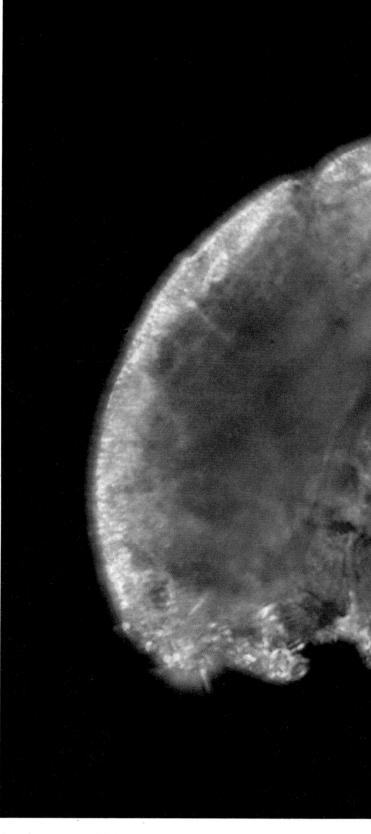

A predatory copepod (left), with a red interior cavity visible, prepares to clamp its forelimbs onto a more primitive zooplankter. The copepod will tear its victim apart and swallow it chunks at a time

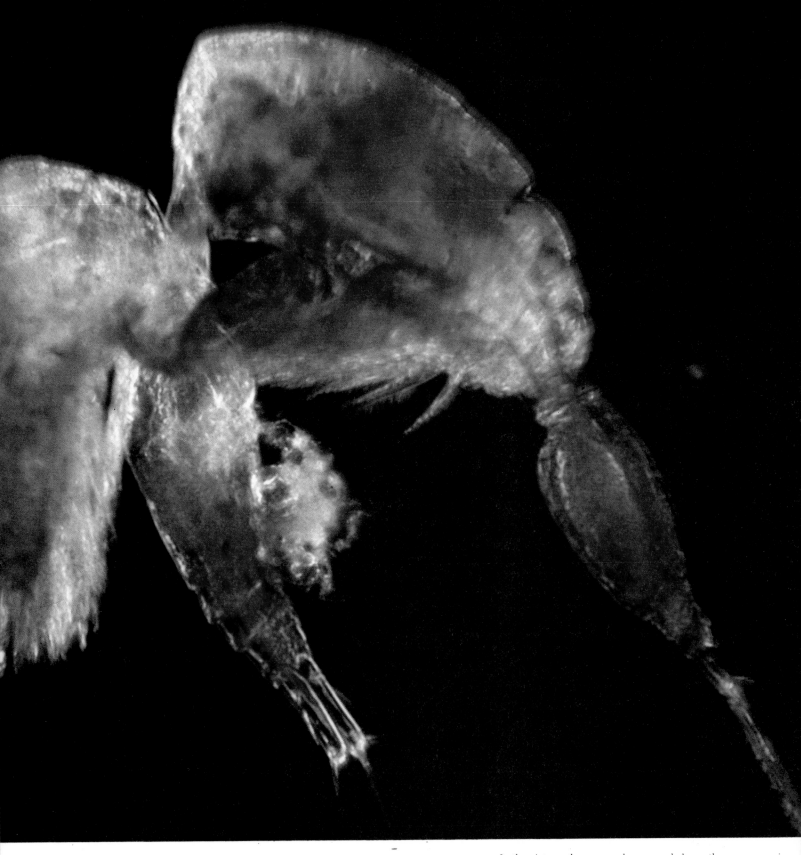

In the picture above, a male copepod clasps the larger female in the act of mating. Sperm is stored in the body of the female copepod until the eggs are ready to be fertilized.

The legs of a streamlined euphausid shrimp are a blur as the creature propels itself forward. Its antennae wave energetically, scouting for a safe path through the dimly lit deep water. The antennae are equipped with sensory cells that are protected by clusters of finely grained hairs.

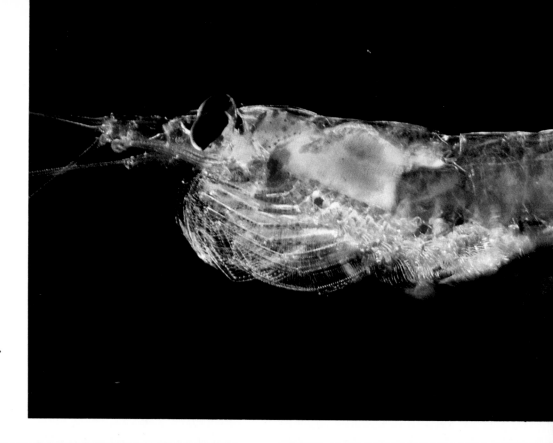

A Gigantocypris (below) retracts into its compact shell. In young specimens, the internal structure and the orange egg clusters seen here are often visible through the transparent carapace. As the organism ages, the transparent shell becomes opaque.

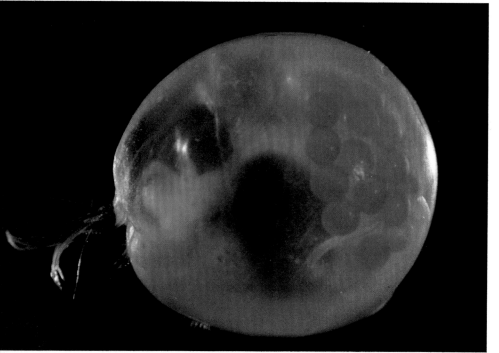

Swimming close to the surface where the red rays of the spectrum penetrate the water, a planktonic prawn glows flamboyantly crimson. In the sunless depths thousands of feet down where the prawn usually swims, its body is protectively shadowy and colorless.

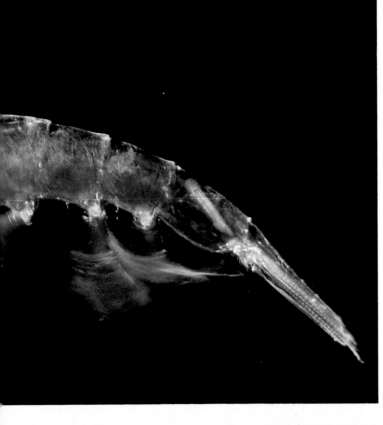

Deepwater Drifters

The planktonic prawns and euphausid shrimps of the ocean's depths have the crustacean's exoskeleton, compound eyes and segmented body, but these free-swimming species depend on special anatomical modifications that allow locomotion in the denser waters of the deep. Their bodies are more streamlined, with well-developed muscles to facilitate movement. The trunk and appendages of the bizarre ostracod *Gigantocypris* are encased in a hinged shell like that of a clam, from which the animal's bristly antennae protrude. In addition to serving as sensory organs, the antennae propel the creature forward efficiently, if awkwardly, through the deeper waters.

Large size in the plankton world is rare. Most ostracods are minute, and although the "giant" *Gigantocypris* averages only three centimeters in length, it is considered a planktonic heavyweight. The euphausid shrimps known as krill are so small a whale may scoop up two or three tons of the minicrustaceans at one feeding.

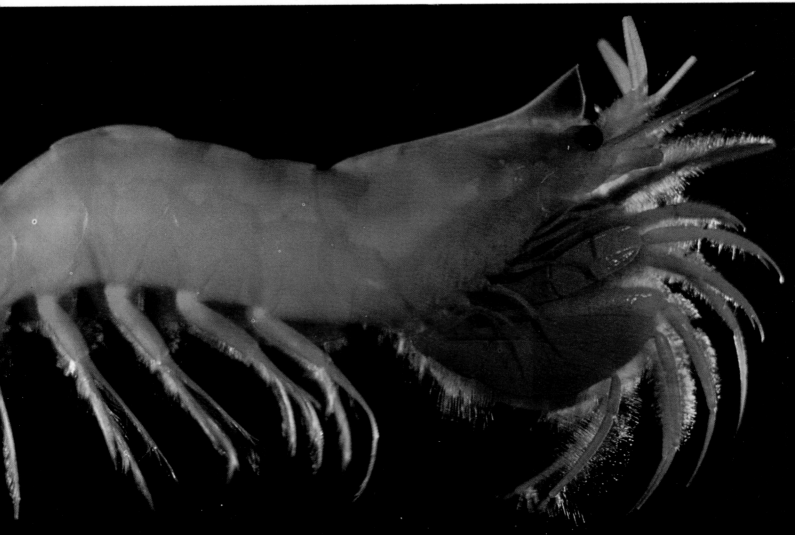

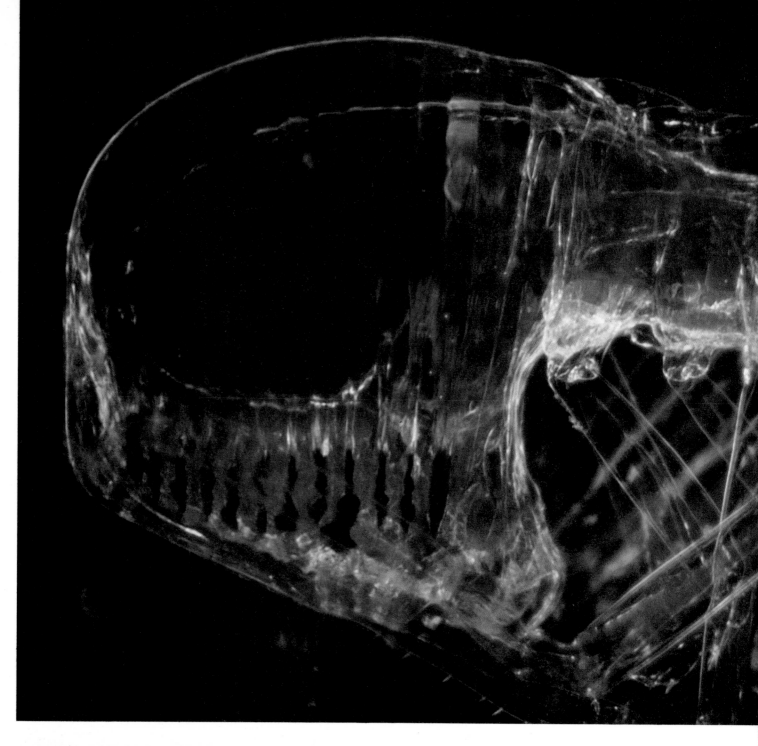

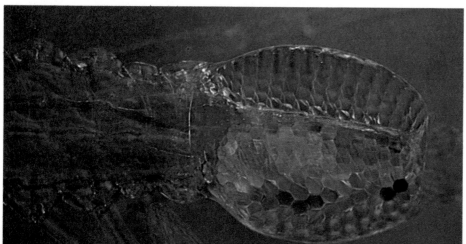

The basic functional unit of a marine amphipod's compound eye (above) consists of light-gathering organs (left) that are covered by translucent corneal tissue; the outer surface of the eye is faceted. These organs transmit light to the inner cones and eventually to the retina. Individual light images are fitted together in a grid effect, producing a large-grained, poorly defined total image.

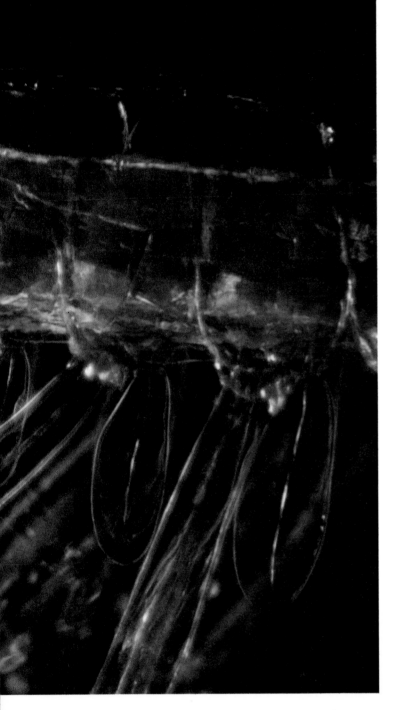

Planktonic Optics

From the simple eye of primitive copepods to the compound eyes of their more highly evolved planktonic relatives to the stalked eyes of some crustacean larvae, planktonic optical organs are surprisingly diverse.

The simple eye of a copepod has a few photoreceptor cells and even fewer lenses; with its single optic nerve, the eye has only enough optical parts to provide sensitivity to light—not enough to receive clearly focused images. The eye thus merely enables the animal to orient itself in relation to a light source.

In groups that have evolved more complex binocular systems—such as the decapods and amphipods—a vestigial simple eye may appear with compound eyes that may be positioned on the sides of the organism's head or perched at the ends of movable eye stalks controlled by special muscles. The appearance and position of such eyes may take bizarre forms: The eyes of a squillid lobster larva, for example, are mounted on disproportionately long stalks that protrude at right angles to the creature's tiny body. And in some oceanic deepwater amphipods the eyes completely envelop the head area.

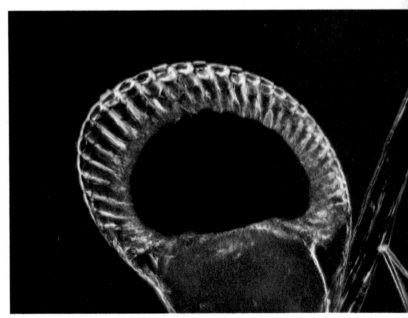

The stalk-mounted eyes of a squillid lobster larva (above) are able to peer about in the clear, sunlit surface waters of the animal's habitat. In some stalk-eyed species, the field of vision can encompass 180 degrees. A copepod (left) has to make do with a single eye set in the middle of its head.

91

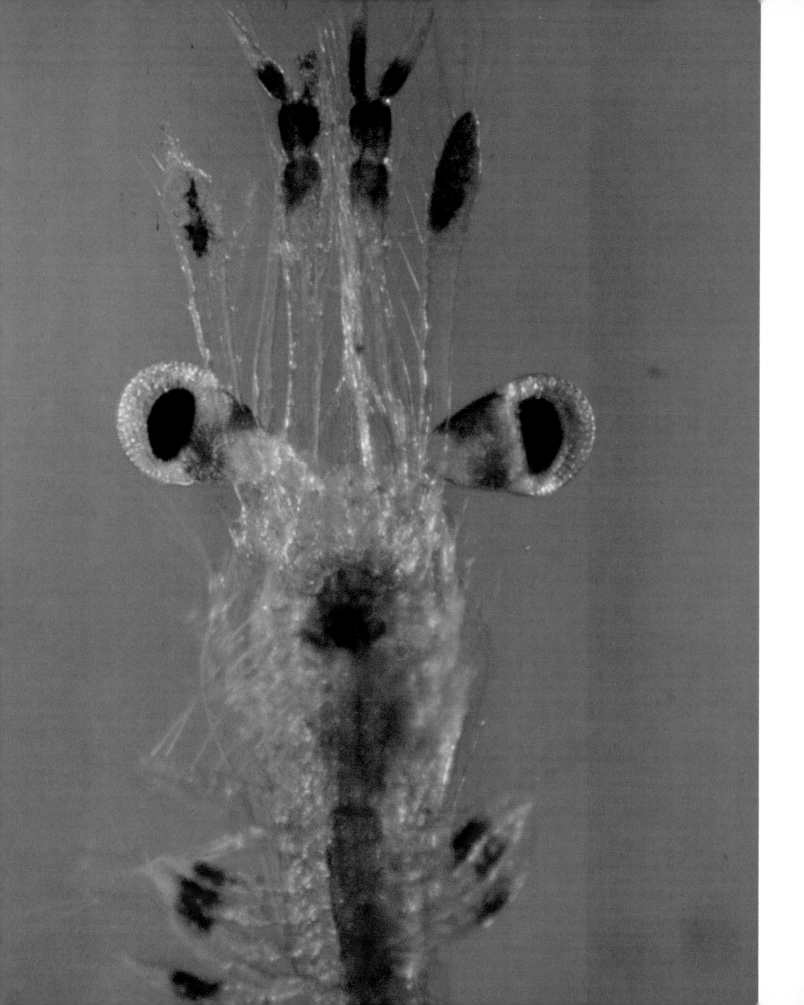

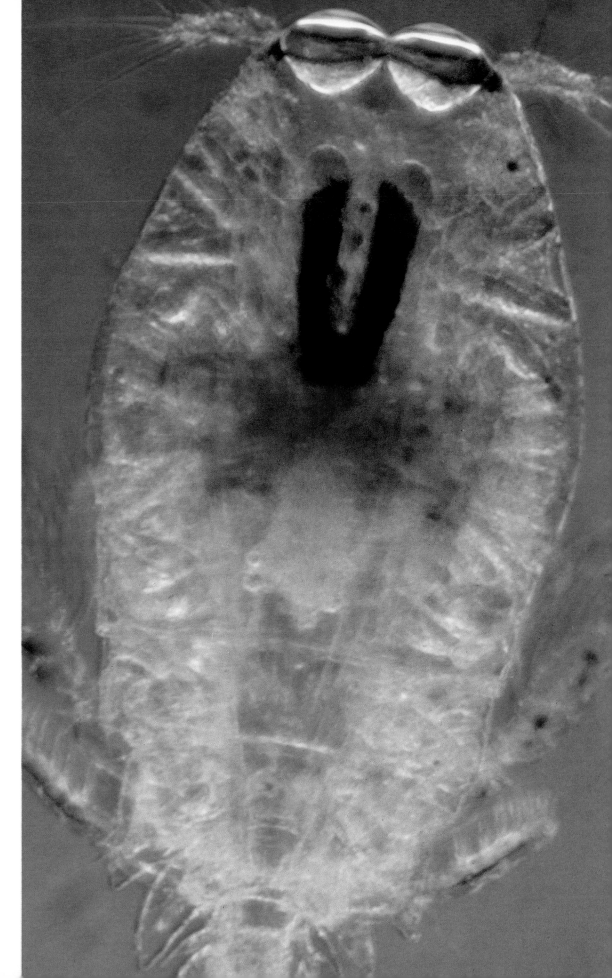

The comparatively large stalked eyes of a decapod larva (left) cover two separate fields of view rather than focusing in on a single image.

Looking like a bespectacled clerk, a copepod (right) displays its simple eye. Scientists are uncertain of the extent to which copepods rely on their limited vision.

Kon-Tiki

by Thor Heyerdahl

In 1947 the Norwegian anthropologist Thor Heyerdahl and five companions traveled across 4,300 miles of the Pacific Ocean on a primitive wood and rope raft called Kon-Tiki. *Securing food each day was a major challenge. In the following passage from Heyerdahl's best-selling account of the journey, he describes the place of plankton in the crew's cuisine.*

In good plankton waters there are thousands in a glassful. More than once persons have starved to death at sea because they did not find fish large enough to be spitted, netted, or hooked. In such cases it has often happened that they have literally been sailing about in strongly diluted, raw fish soup. If, in addition to hooks and nets, they had had a utensil for straining the soup they were sitting in, they would have found a nourishing meal—plankton. Some day in the future, perhaps, men will think of harvesting plankton from the sea to the same extent as now they harvest grain on land. A single grain is of no use, either, but in large quantities it becomes food.

The marine biologist Dr. A. D. Bajkov told us of plankton and sent us a fishing net which was suited to the creatures we were to catch. The "net" was a silk net with almost three thousand meshes per square inch. It was sewn in the shape of a funnel with a circular mouth behind an iron ring, eighteen inches across, and was towed behind the raft. Just as in other kinds of fishing, the catch varied with time and place. Catches diminished as the sea grew warmer farther west, and we got the best results at night, because many species seemed to go deeper down into the water when the sun was shining.

If we had no other way of whiling away time on board the raft, there would have been entertainment enough in lying with our noses in the plankton net. Not for the sake of the smell, for that was bad. Nor because the sight was appetizing, for it looked a horrible mess. But because, if we spread the plankton out on a board and examined each of the little creatures separately with the naked eye, we had before us fantastic shapes and colors in unending variety.

Most of them were tiny shrimplike crustaceans (*copepods*) or fish ova floating loose, but there were also larvae of fish and shellfish, curious miniature crabs in all colors, jellyfish, and an endless variety of small creatures which might have been taken from Walt Disney's *Fantasia*. Some looked like fringed, fluttering spooks cut out of cellophane paper, while others resembled tiny red-beaked birds with hard shells instead of feathers. There was no end to Nature's extravagant inventions in the plankton world; a surrealistic artist might well own himself bested here.

Where the cold Humboldt Current turned west south of the Equator, we could pour several pounds of plankton porridge out of the bag every few hours. The plankton lay packed together like cake in colored layers—brown, red, gray, and green according to the different fields of plankton through which we had passed. At night, when there was phosphorescence about, it was like hauling in a bag of sparkling jewels. But, when we got hold of it, the pirates' treasure turned into millions of tiny glittering shrimps and phosphorescent fish larvae that glowed in the dark like a heap of live coals. When we poured them into a bucket, the squashy mess ran out like a magic gruel composed of glowworms. Our night's catch looked as nasty at close quarters as it had been pretty at long range. And, bad as it smelled, it tasted correspondingly good if one just plucked up courage and put a spoonful of it into one's mouth. If this consisted of many dwarf shrimps, it tasted like shrimp paste, lobster, or crab. If it was mostly deep-sea fish ova, it tasted like caviar and now and then like oysters.

The inedible vegetable plankton were either so small that they washed away with the water through the meshes of the net, or they were so large that we could pick them up with our fingers. "Snags" in the dish were single jellylike coelenterates like glass balloons and jellyfish about half an inch long. These were bitter and had to be thrown away. Otherwise everything could be eaten, either as it was or cooked in fresh water as gruel or soup. Tastes differ. Two men on board thought plankton tasted delicious, two thought they were quite good, and for two the sight of them was more than enough. From a nutrition standpoint they stand on a level with the larger shellfish, and, spiced and properly prepared, they can certainly be a first-class dish for all who like marine food.

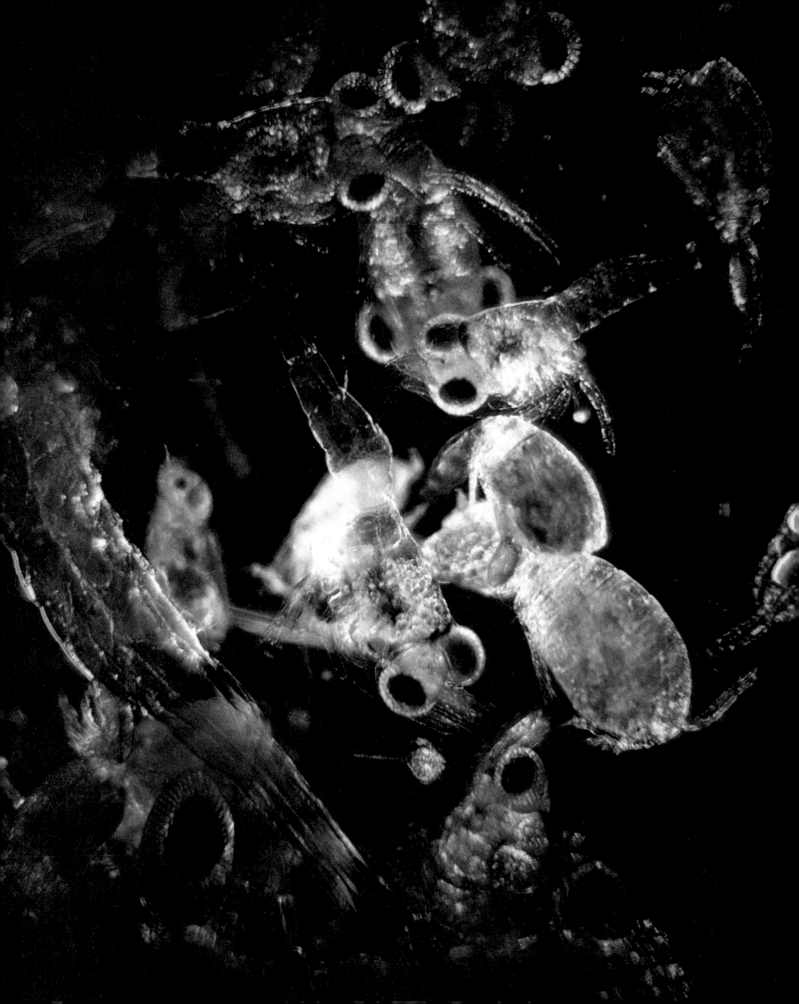

The vibrating tail fin of a sagittid arrowworm propels the creature through the water. Lateral fins provide equilibrium and keep the slender, cylindrical body from keeling over.

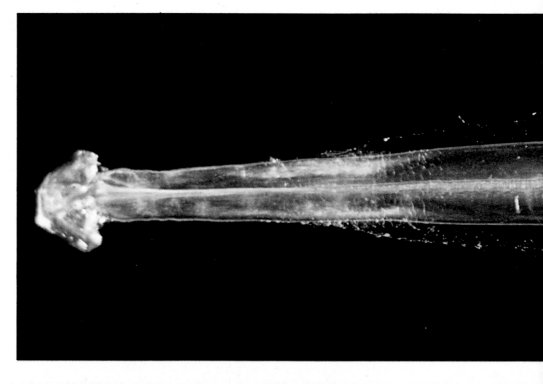

A solitary pelagic salp (below) swims by means of a primitive pumping system: It draws water into its mouth and then expels it from a posterior opening. Circular muscle bands perform the pumping action.

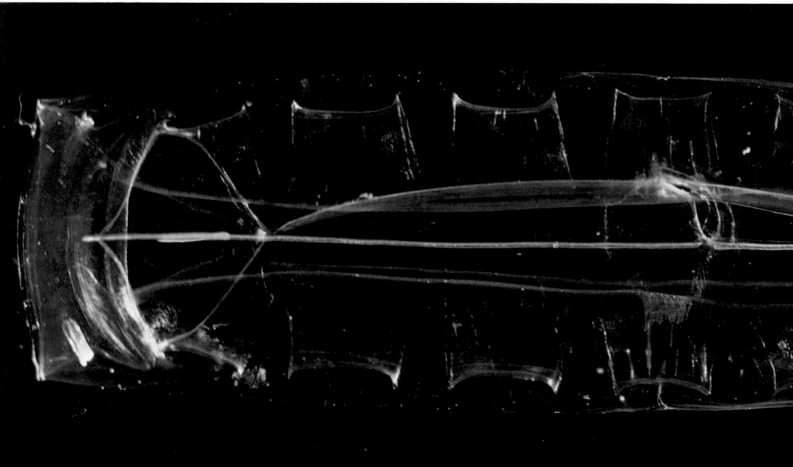

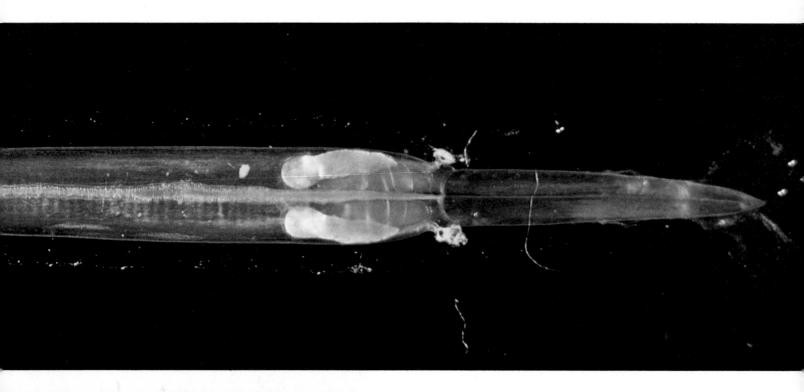

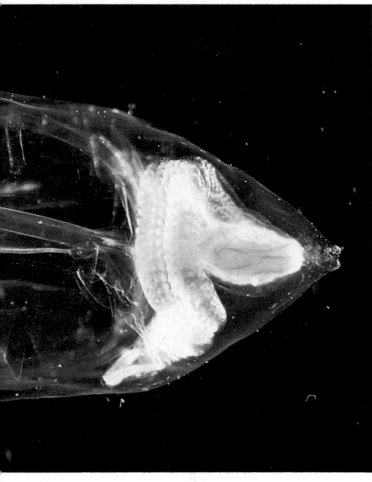

Higher Orders

Among the more complex of the marine invertebrates are the arrowworms and salps. Arrowworms represent a distinctive phylum—Chaetognatha. Aggressive and predatory, they have a definite arrow shape and are correspondingly swift.

Arrowworms hang suspended in the water until they are ready to strike; attacking, they fan their tail fins to gain momentum, then dart forward to dispatch an unwary copepod or drifting larva. A number of spiny bristles surround the organism's mouth region, whiskery projections that clamp down on prey, acting as pincers to hold the victim still so it can be swept into the gullet. A loosely draped fold in the arrowworm's body wall forms a hood that can enclose the head region, including the spines. In motion, this reduces the friction of the water against the body and lends speed to the attack.

Arrowworms are hermaphroditic: Sperm and eggs are produced in the same animal at the same time, and some species reproduce by self-fertilization. The salps, among the most advanced invertebrates, are also hermaphroditic —but male and female gonads do not mature simultaneously in an individual. Two organisms must fertilize each other in order to produce a third—a so-called nurse organism that in turn reproduces asexually to generate a new brood of salps.

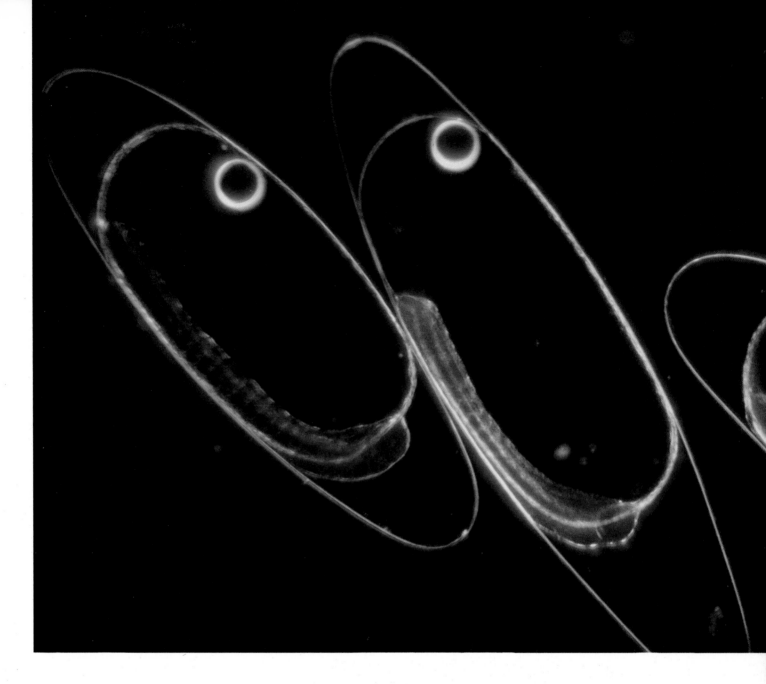

Safety in Numbers

Many marine fishes shed their eggs in open waters near the sea's surface, but unlike the variety of plankters that have a modicum of mobility, these pelagic fish eggs must depend totally on the ocean currents for motion and for the distribution of the species.

The defenseless embryos, enclosed in their egg membranes and feeding on the nutrients of the rich yolk within the egg, stay afloat by means of droplets of oil contained in the egg, which also balance their weight; they develop in their incubation chambers as they drift along.

The larvae that hatch out of the protective eggs are also temporarily planktonic. Some species have control over the direction of their courses as larvae and are able to prey upon other zooplankters. For several weeks these larvae feed on small organisms such as copepods, building up their strength for life as adults.

But during this highly vulnerable period, the larvae also are prey to a variety of other larger and more self-sufficient creatures such as the comb jellies, medusae, siphonophores and arrowworms, and only by the sheer vastness of their numbers are they able to compensate for the high mortality rate.

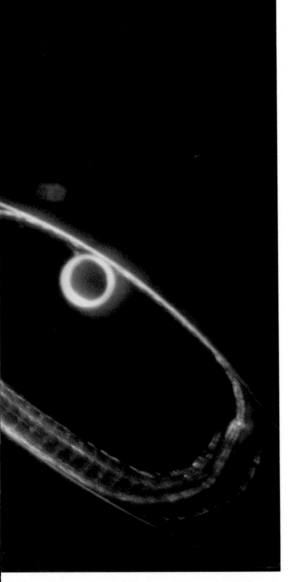

A trio of pelagic fish eggs (left) have a surreal look. Fat globules inside keep the eggs afloat. An egg membrane (below) encloses an embryo, eyeless in an early developmental stage.

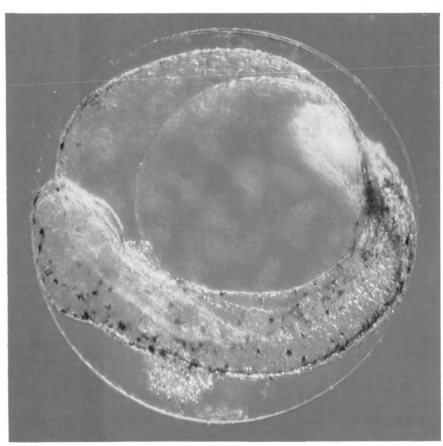

A fish larva (below) cruises its territory for food. Many larvae remain attached to the yolk sacs after they leave the eggs, and thus have a ready food supply for a few days.

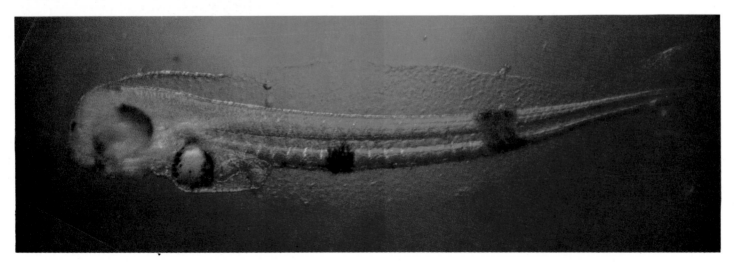

Larval Forms

During certain seasons, the sea's nutrient-rich waters become a vast nursery, and nature has rarely been more inventive than in the fanciful but utilitarian forms it has designed for its immature life. Much like caterpillars that metamorphose into butterflies, these larval creatures often bear little resemblance to their parents. Some look like tiny glass beads or cones with hair belts, whirling through the water like miniature tops. Others resemble gelatinous flecks with enormous earlike flaps or greatly reduced versions of shapes that mimic plumed hats, fringed mushrooms and crumpled cellophane. It almost strains credulity that these tiny organisms, changing both their appearance and their habits, will mature into burrowing worms, creeping starfish or even such permanently anchored residents of the ocean as bryozoans and barnacles.

Only a few groups of larvae—most notably of such crustaceans as copepods—will drift as part of the plankton for the rest of their lives. Most larvae are sent aloft as eggs by bottom dwellers so that they can take temporary advantage of the nourishing layers of plankton near the surface. In much the same way that plants use the wind to disperse their seeds, the inhabitants of the ocean's floor release their buoyant eggs into the wandering currents in enormous quantities—millions a year in the case of a spawning female oyster or starfish. Most of the tiny eggs are quickly gobbled up by hungry fish and other predators. But more than enough hatch to fill the sea with a multitude of surviving specks of life.

During the days or weeks that the larvae are afloat, they share many characteristics with the permanent members of the plankton as well as with one another. For protection, they are transparent so that they blend with the water. And to stay afloat, most are lightweight and have rings or bands of fine hairs known as cilia, which whip through the water like miniature oars.

Before many of these larvae can assume an adult mode of life, they must undergo a complete transformation. For some, the transition, or metamorphosis, from larva to adult is gradual. A flatworm larva, for example, starts out as a simple sphere that soon sprouts a series of armlike ciliated lobes, and then slowly begins to flatten out and elongate into its mature form. Some other larval worms, by contrast, carry their hindquarters in a cavity formed by the folding over of the front segments. When the young worm is heavy enough to begin its descent to the ocean floor, it undergoes a dramatic coming of age: It straightens itself out in a matter of seconds, much like a parachute shooting out of its pack.

Although just as minuscule and delicately transparent, the larvae of some of the sea's advanced invertebrates are more readily indentifiable as members of their group in the animal kingdom. Of these animals, the larvae of shrimps, lobsters, crabs, crayfish and other crustaceans are the most representative.

As hatchlings, most of the tiny kite-shaped creatures look enough alike to make their specific parentage mysterious to all but the most skilled biologist. But their translucent shells and jointed legs are dead giveaways that they are crustaceans. And as the larvae continually shed their outgrown external skeletons and manufacture new ones, they add more legs and body sections until at last they are complete miniature adults.

One crustacean, however, had scientists confused for generations. While goose barnacle larvae also resemble their crustacean kin, an adult barnacle hidden inside the calcareous shell that it secretes is so well disguised that it was once thought to be some kind of mollusk—perhaps an odd kind of clam—and unrelated to its larvae. Another baffling disparity between larval and adult forms is offered by the sea squirts. Stationary on the bottom as adults, sea squirt larvae swim freely, look like tiny tadpoles and, surprisingly, like their relatives the salps, share an anatomical characteristic with vertebrates.

The most intriguing of all the sea's youngsters, however, may well belong to the species in which major parts of the larva are expendable. Within the free-swimming helmet-shaped pilidium larva of a nemertean, a young worm develops around the mouth and stomach at the central core, and the miniature nemertean worm, as it emerges, devours the outer larval tissue that has enclosed it, and then sinks to the sea's bottom.

A similar but even more complicated transformation occurs among the echinoderms, a group that includes starfish, brittle stars, sea urchins and sea cucumbers. In the partially developed larva of a starfish, a large fluid-filled sac balloons out of the left side. The emergent form develops a mouth, nervous system and other vital organs, and soon the developing starfish begins to absorb more and more of the larva from which it sprouted, eventually consuming it completely. As one noted zoologist has observed, "The birth of Eve is no stranger story."

Larva of slipper lobster

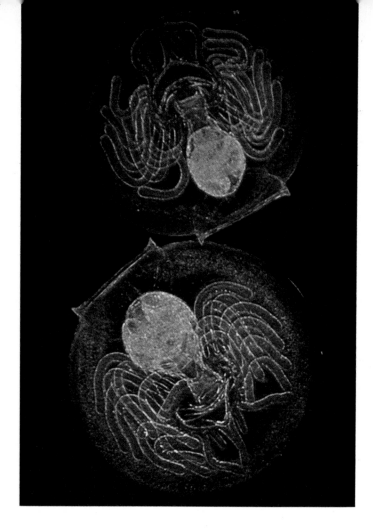

Inside their transparent shells, brachiopod larvae (left) propel themselves by means of beating cilia. An adult brachiopod, attached to a marine plant·stem (below), continually secretes additional rings of shell as it grows, but it rarely reaches more than three inches in its lifetime.

A horseshoe crab embryo (below) develops inside an egg into a trilobite larva. Horseshoe crabs are not crabs; they are related to spiders and scorpions. When female horseshoe crabs lay eggs (right), males swarm around, vying for a chance to fertilize them.

The Ancient Mariners

Brachiopods and horseshoe crabs represent very ancient lineages, and both groups of animals are related to some of the oldest known marine fossils. Fossil remains of some brachiopods very similar to species living today have been found in rocks about 500 million years old, and horseshoe crabs have existed virtually unchanged for about 380 million years.

When the larvae of a horseshoe crab hatch and crawl out from beneath the sand where the eggs were buried, they more closely resemble an extinct arthropod called a trilobite than they do a horseshoe crab, and they are referred to as trilobite larvae. The larvae are able to burrow in the sand and swim near the shore, and within a short time they develop into miniature horseshoe crabs. The planktonic larvae of brachiopods, depending on the species, may sink to the sea floor and attach themselves by a stalk while metamorphosing and secreting a shell; or they may, while still swimming, develop a shell whose weight causes them to sink to the bottom, where the adults then burrow in the sediment on the ocean floor.

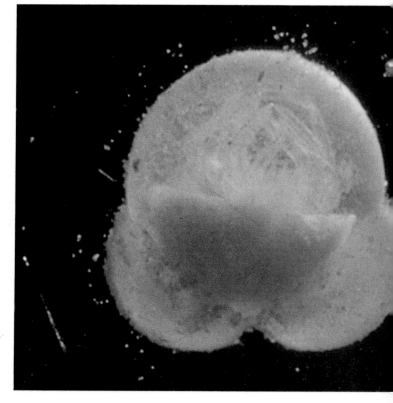

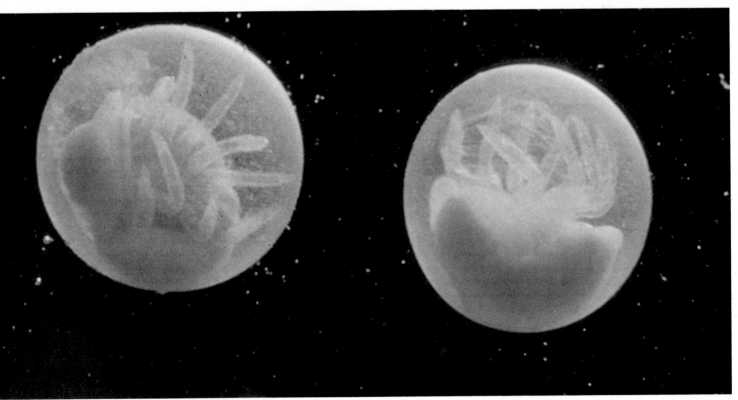

Seashore Colonials

Looking like a mossy carpet, colonies of microscopic bryozoans cover the surfaces of plants and rocks in the shallow waters near the seashore. Each individual bryozoan, or zooid, lives within a chamber, frequently calcareous, that it secretes and that is attached to those of its neighbors. In order to feed, the zooid pokes out an anterior disk with waving ciliated tentacles that send specks of planktonic food into its mouth; if disturbed, the creature withdraws into its private domain.

A bryozoan colony enlarges by asexual reproduction, usually at the edges of the colony, where there is space for expansion. Since individual bryozoans usually live only a few weeks, a zooid produced by budding may also take over any empty space left by a dead neighbor. An entirely new colony is initiated through sexual reproduction: The hermaphroditic zooids produce pinpoint-sized larvae and send them drifting off into the sea.

The larva, called a cyphonautes, has bands of cilia on its triangular-shaped "wings" that keep its body afloat. When the appropriate time in its development arrives, the larva settles on the bottom, and after metamorphosis, the primary zooid—appropriately called an ancestrula—begins to produce other zooids by budding.

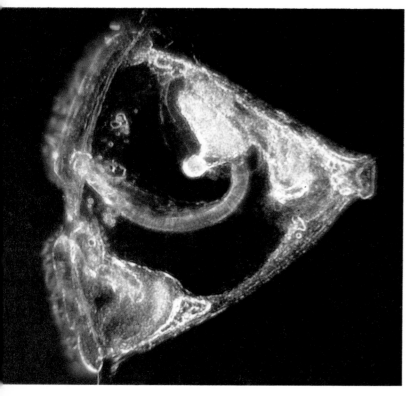

A bryozoan larva (left) has a simple gut between triangular plates edged with cilia. It is constructed for balance, and the apex of the triangle is always the leading edge.

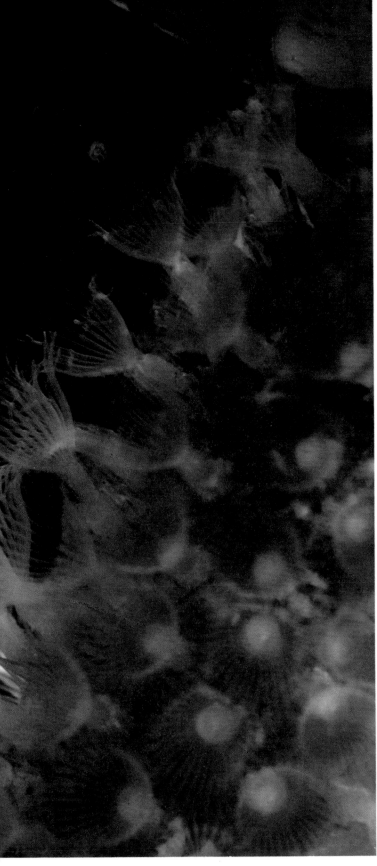

Magnified slightly, a colony of bryozoans encrusts an aquatic plant (below). Under extreme magnification, an area of a colony (overleaf) of a different bryozoan species resembles a fisherman's net. Brown areas in a square indicate that one of the short-lived individuals has died.

Highly magnified, a bryozoan colony (above) creates currents with the cilia on the tentacles of its zooids. Organisms such as diatoms are trapped by the tentacles and scooped into open mouths.

The Müller's larva of a polyclad (below. left) has ciliated lobes near its posterior end that keep it afloat. As the larva develops, the lobes are gradually absorbed until, in the flat disklike stage on the right, it sinks to the bottom.

An adult polyclad (right) lurks on the sea's floor. The bright-yellow pattern visible through the worm's transparent epidermis is its alimentary canal. Like its larva, the worm has only one orifice—its mouth.

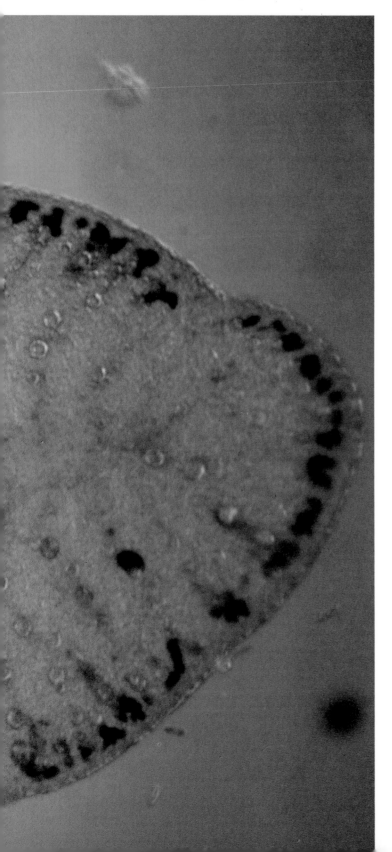

Leaflike Worms

Of the three classes of flatworms in the phylum Platyhelminthes, only one, Turbellaria, is comprised of free-living species rather than parasitic species. The largest of the turbellarians are the polyclad flatworms, which can reach a length of several inches. Usually shaped like a leaf, a polyclad has a mouth on its ventral surface that leads to a branching alimentary canal (polyclad means "many branches"). Creeping about on the floor of the ocean, polyclads feed voraciously on other invertebrates such as sedentary oysters and barnacles.

Most turbellarians are hermaphroditic and reproduce by cross fertilization, but some also reproduce asexually by fission. Only certain species of polyclads, however, have a free-swimming form, called a Müller's larva, after its 19th Century discoverer. The larva develops eight lobes fringed with long cilia that enable it to swim for a few days; then with its lobes absorbed and with a distinct resemblance to an adult polyclad it sinks to the ocean's bottom where it completes the transition.

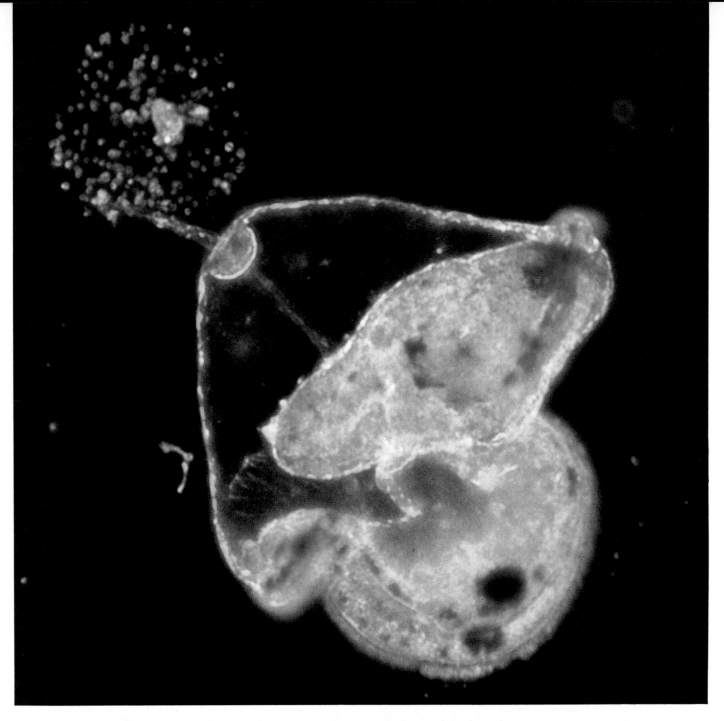

An Armed Elastic Ribbon

The slender marine worms of the phylum Nemertina can be as short as one millimeter or as long as 90 feet. Also called ribbon worms, nemerteans can, like elastic bands, stretch and contract considerably. The worms have a long, tubular proboscis that can be extended and is provided either with sharp spines or with gland cells containing a sticky secretion for catching prey. If broken off, the proboscis regenerates, a capacity that the worms also demonstrate with almost any other part of their bodies.

The sexes are separate in most species, and eggs are fertilized after the female sheds them in the water. In some nemerteans there is a swimming and feeding larval stage that disperses the species. In this stage, the so-called pilidium larva undergoes a dramatic metamorphosis: Its central area, containing the mouth and gut, develops into a young worm that emerges from within the rest of the larva, which it consumes. It then drifts to the ocean floor, where it completes the transformation into an adult nemertean.

A helmet-shaped pilidium larva (left) has a tuft of cilia on top that serves as a sense organ. Within the pilidium, through a complex metamorphosis, a young nemertean worm will develop.

A nemertean worm (above) glides along the ocean floor seeking prey such as annelid worms. Sensing a victim nearby, the nemertean shown below unfurls its proboscis in preparation for an attack.

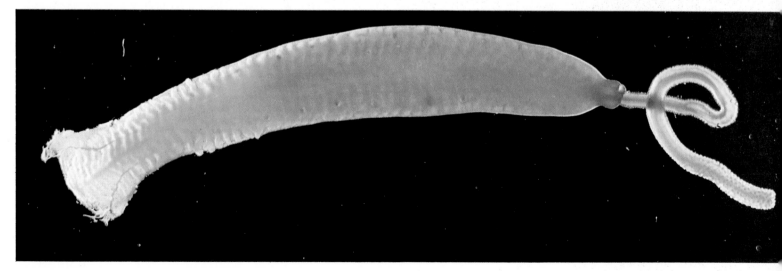

Urchins to Be

Sea urchins, or Echinoidea, are familiar members of the phylum Echinodermata, and they occupy a wide variety of marine habitats, ranging from shallow waters near the shore to the ocean's depths. The sea urchins are characterized by their spines, in some, long and needle sharp; in others, as thick as a pencil; and in still others, very short and covering the animal like fur. Like other echinoderms the sea urchin has a larva with little resemblance to the adult (overleaf). A major difference is that the larva is bilaterally symmetrical, with matching left and right sides and the ability to move only forward; the adult is radially symmetrical and can move in any direction.

The bottom-living adult sea urchin, however, has only a moderate ability to move about. It is the larva with its long ciliated arms that can transport a future urchin and disperse the species sufficiently throughout its habitat so that overcrowding of the habitat and extreme competition for food are avoided.

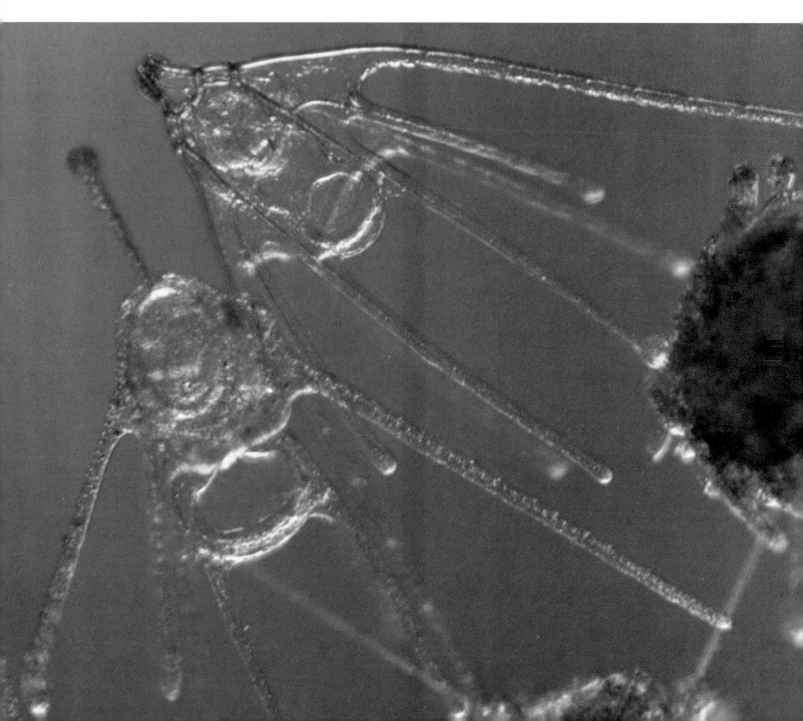

The body of an adult sea urchin (right) is almost hidden under the protection of its thick spines. Despite its appearance, the sea urchin is able to move with the tube feet that are located on its underside.

The sea urchin larvae appearing on the left-hand side of the picture below will metamorphose into young sea urchins like those on the right side.

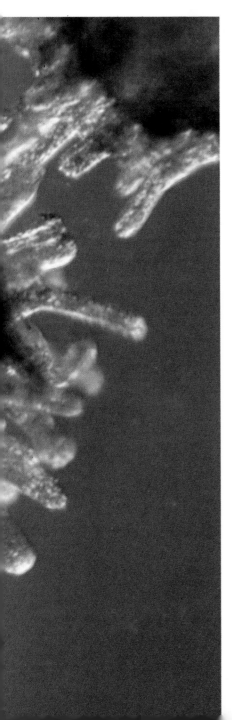

Swept along by long ciliated larval arms, an ophiopluteus larva of a brittle star sails past a sponge larva. The pluteus is the stage of development in which metamorphosis into a brittle star occurs.

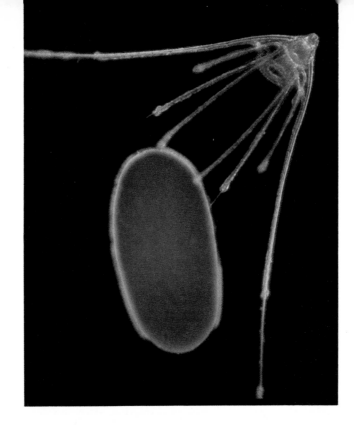

In a more advanced stage, the young brittle star coexists with remaining pluteus tissues (below). The star will soon absorb the rest of the pluteus.

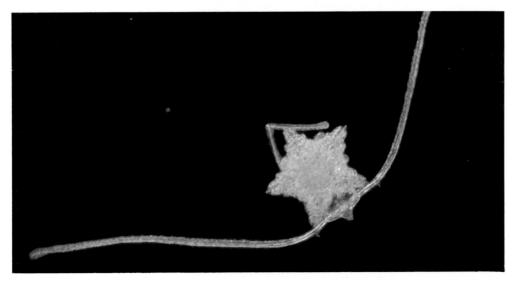

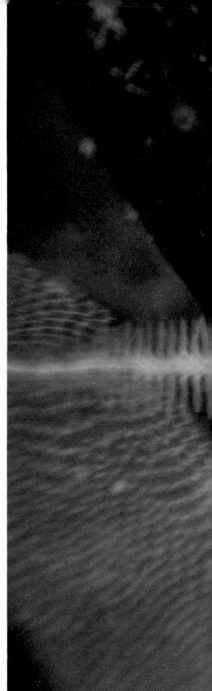

The immature brittle star at right has sunk to the ocean bottom, having absorbed the pluteus from which it emerged.

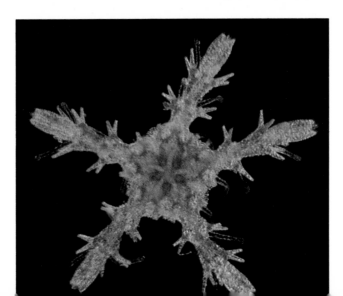

The five flexible arms of an adult brittle star (above) propel it with a rapid rowing motion along the bottom. More active than its starfish relatives, the brittle star often breaks off its arms. However, it is able to regenerate body parts and can also discard pieces of its arms when in danger.

Artful Larvae

The brittle stars are echinoderms that tend to creep along the ocean floor. Like most other members of the phylum, they cast their eggs and sperm so that they can float freely and meet for fertilization. The release of either eggs or sperm seems to trigger the release of the other. From a floating brittle star egg an early embryonic form known as a blastula emerges and develops into a larva called an ophiopluteus: Ophiuroidea is the class to which brittle stars belong, and the word pluteus derives from the Greek for "artist's easel." The pluteus larva, however, is not actually the future adult brittle star, but merely temporary transport for the incipient adult.

Out of the left side of the ophiopluteus larva bulges a sac; equipped with its own separate mouth and nervous system, the sac begins to take on the five-armed shape of the adult brittle star. During this metamorphosis, the developing brittle star absorbs the remaining larval tissue and then sinks to the ocean floor.

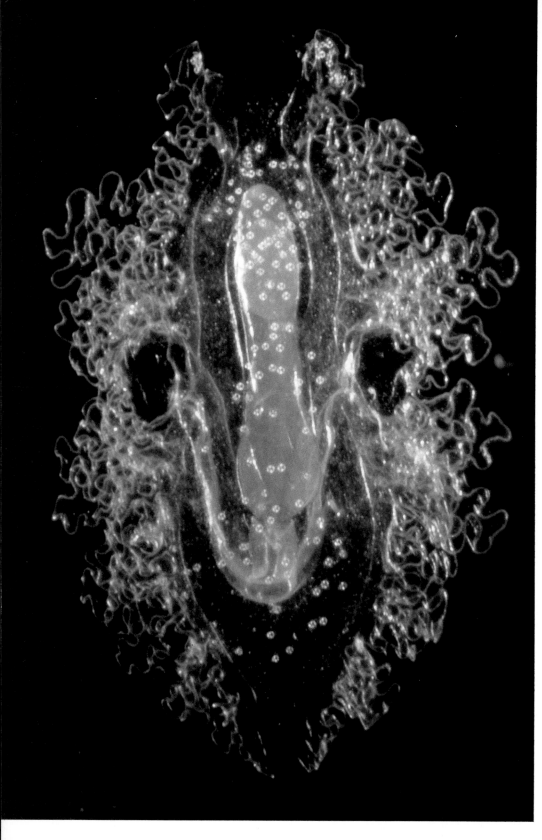

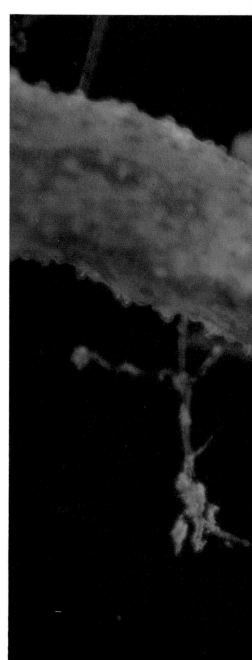

The larva of a sea cucumber (one is isolated at left; a group appears at right) has ossicles, calcereous structures embedded in the animal's "skin." In this larval form, called an auricularia, bands of cilia on its surface keep the larva afloat.

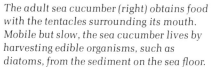

The adult sea cucumber (right) obtains food with the tentacles surrounding its mouth. Mobile but slow, the sea cucumber lives by harvesting edible organisms, such as diatoms, from the sediment on the sea floor.

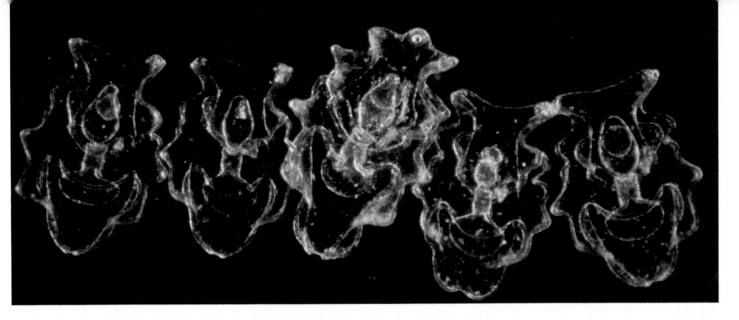

Barnacle Phases

Barnacles, with their tendency to attach themselves to boat hulls, have always been a maritime nuisance. Yet for centuries no one knew exactly what kind of animal they were. As late as the 16th Century it was believed that the goose barnacle, with its egg-shaped shells hanging on a fleshy stalk, actually produced geese. And until the 19th Century adult barnacles were wrongly considered to be mollusks. Then, in 1828, the British physician and naturalist S. Vaughan Thompson observed free-swimming crustacean larvae develop into adult barnacles—shrimplike creatures that are permanently attached to an object and imprisoned inside their shells.

Further investigations revealed that the barnacle larva, or nauplius, passes through six stages of molting and then undergoes a transition into a cyprid larval stage—so named because it resembles another major group of crustaceans, the *Cypris* ostracods. The cyprid larva has a thin bivalved shell, six pairs of legs and two pairs of antennae. It swims around for a short time and then cements itself with its antennae to a suitable surface. The cyprid larva metamorphoses into the adult barnacle, which secretes a set of calcareous plates that protect it from most predators.

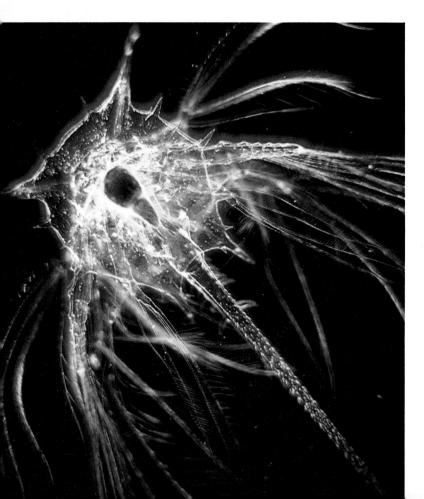

Goose barnacles (above) are attached to driftwood by the flexible stalks at their anterior end. Inside the partly open plates of their shells they wave bristly legs that direct food into their mouths.

A nauplius larva of a barnacle propels itself through the water with a set of its appendages (left). Many crustaceans have a similar nauplius stage: The word comes from the Greek for "sailor."

Still mobile, as shown at right, a cyprid larva develops from the nauplius. Its antennae, which contain cement glands, become a stalk when the larva attaches itself and metamorphoses.

Sea squirt larvae look like tadpoles
and undulate like fish. The
notochords that give support to their
tails disappear when the larvae
metamorphose into adult sea squirts.

A Backbone Blueprint

Adult sea squirts often resemble nothing more than a simple rubbery sack with two openings. Yet sea squirts are so definitely linked to vertebrate animals that zoologists place them in the same phylum as human beings—Chordata. The major link is the notochord, an elastic rod that occurs in the free-swimming tadpole-like larvae of sea squirts and in vertebrates; however, in the latter the notochord is usually replaced during embryonic development by the vertebrae forming the backbone. When the sea squirt larva becomes an adult, the notochord disappears, but zoologists have speculated that in the early stages of evolution some sea squirt larvae may have matured while retaining their mobility and their notochord—and thus evolved into an ancestral vertebrate form.

Most sea squirts are hermaphrodites that release fertilized eggs in the sea. The developing embryo elongates and the notochord is formed. The notochord gives skeletal support to the larva and makes its fishlike locomotion possible. Above the notochord is a hollow neural tube that leads to a simple brain. The often mouthless larva does not feed, and after a brief time it settles on a surface and secretes a cementing adhesive. Then it absorbs its tail, its notochord and neural tube, and assuming a sort of U shape, it becomes an adult sea squirt.

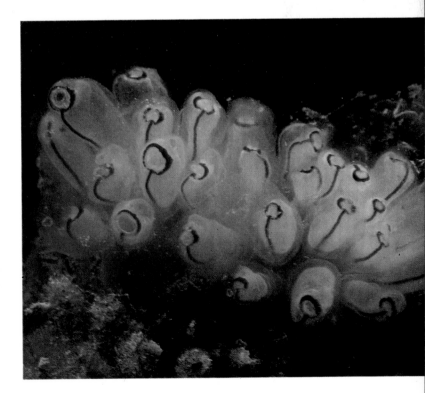

Attached to the ocean floor in shallow water, the sea squirts at right feed on plankton. The currents created by cilia sweep food into one orifice of the sea squirt's body; water and waste exit from the squirt's other opening.

Tornaria larva of an enteropneust worm (right)

Ephyra larva of a scyphozoan coelenterate

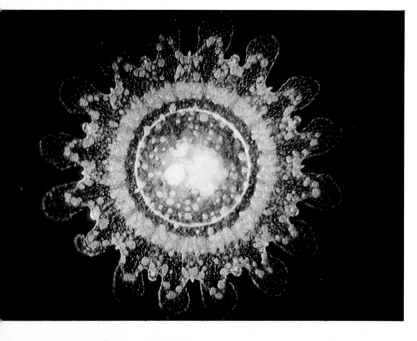

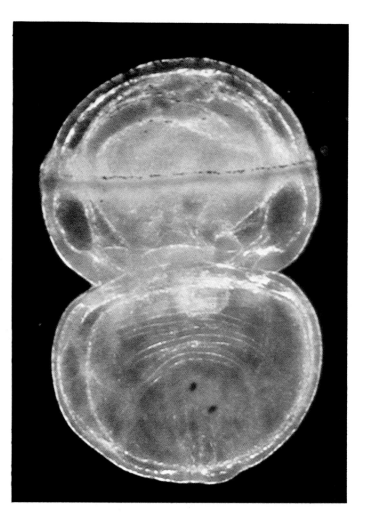

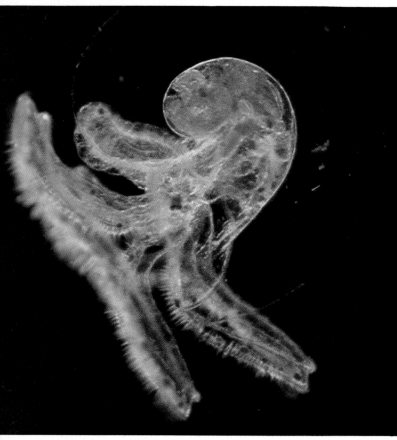

Veliger larva of a gastropod mollusk

Specks of Life

Although all must accomplish the same mission of survival, the minute larvae of many aquatic animals, such as those shown here, are confoundingly disparate—not only from one another but from their adult forms. Determining the ultimate taxonomical destination of a larva has long presented challenges to biologists: Scientists occasionally mistake the larva of a familiar aquatic animal for an undiscovered kind of adult plankter. Many of the names used for larval and other reproductive stages—for example, tornaria and ephyra—were originally invented to describe what were thought to be "new" species of plankton.

The development of a larva into an adult must be observed to determine its true heritage and destiny. However, maintaining the fragile young larvae in the laboratory is difficult, and many a mysterious form among the multitudes of larvae examined each year remains unidentified for some time.

Larva of an annelid worm (left)

Actinotroch larva of a phoronid

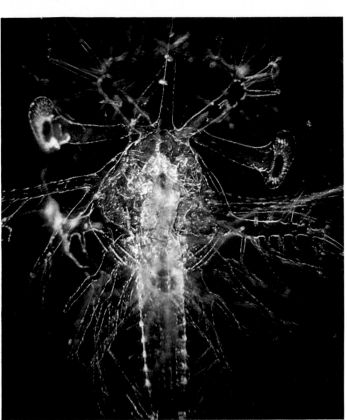

Larva of a Sergestes prawn (left)

A brilliantly hued microscopic larva (overleaf) with a halo of cilia was taken in a tow net off the coast of Jamaica in 1967. It has still not been positively identified.

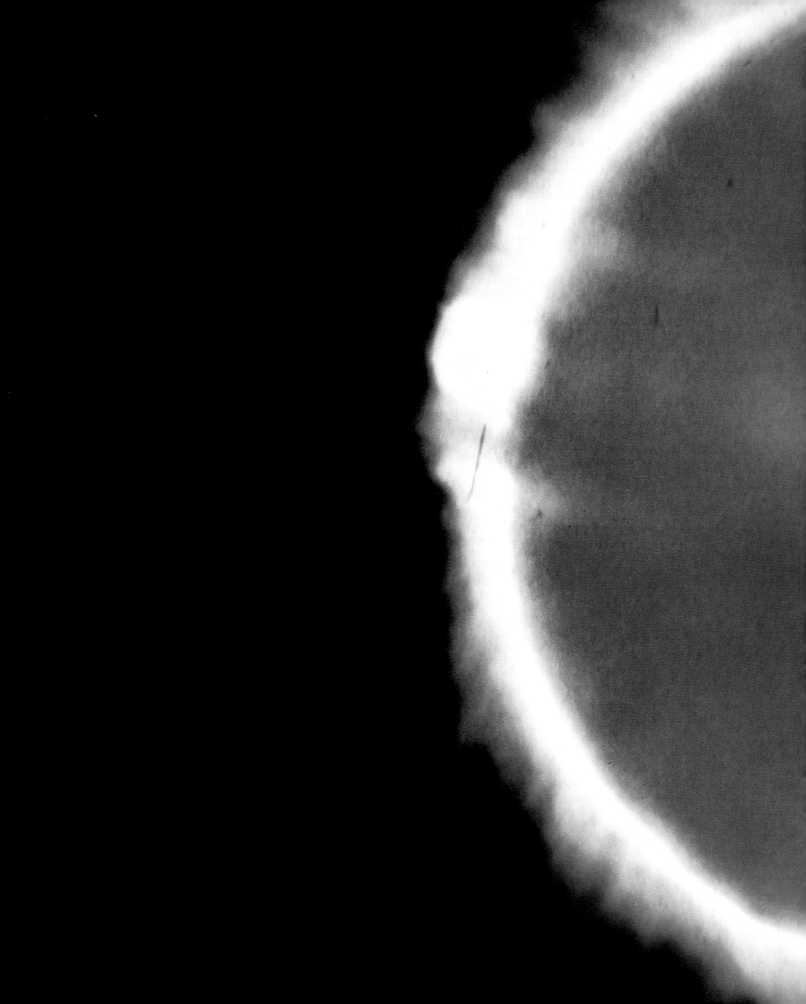

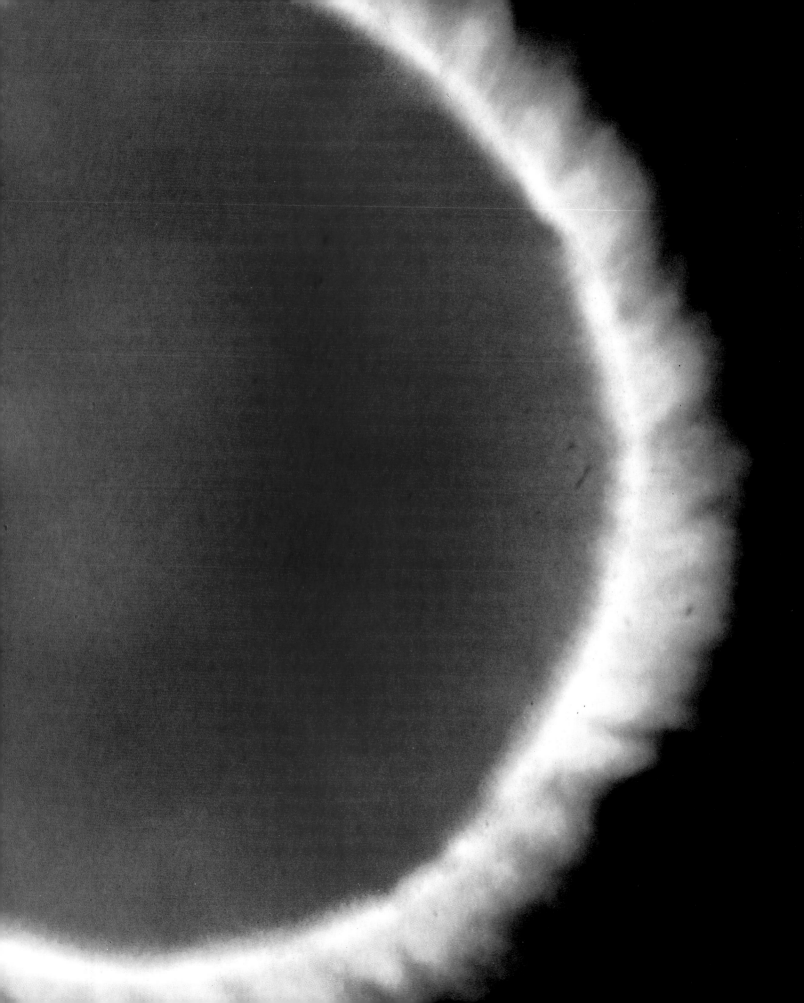

Credits

All photographs in this book, including the one on the cover, are from Oxford Scientific Films, except those listed below.

16—W. Amos, Bruce Coleman, Inc. 24–25 (top)—O.S.F., Bruce Coleman, Inc. 30–31—W. Amos, B.C., Inc. 41 (top, left)—O.S.F., B.C., Inc. 49 (bottom)—W. Amos, B.C., Inc. 58–59—K. Sandved, B.C., Inc. 67 (top)—W. Amos, B.C., Inc.; (bottom)—W. Amos, B.C., Inc. 68 (bottom, left)—W. Amos, B.C., Inc. 71—W. Amos, B.C., Inc. 102–103 (bottom)—W. Amos, B.C., Inc., 103 (top)—J. Carmichael, B.C., Inc.

The photographs on the endpapers are used courtesy of the Time-Life Picture Agency, Russ Kinne and Stephen Dalton of Photo Researchers, Inc., and Nina Leen.

The film sequence on page 8 is from "Giants of the Northern Deep," a program in the Time-Life Television series *Wild, Wild World of Animals*.

THE ILLUSTRATIONS: The illustration on page 14 is by Constance Timm. The mezzotint on page 16 is by Verkdje, courtesy of the Museum of the History of Science, Oxford University. The painting on pages 36–37 is by Neil R. Anderson. The painting on pages 54–55 is by Catherine Siracusa. The illustration on pages 74–75 is by John Groth.

Bibliography

NOTE: An asterisk at left means that a paperback volume is also available.

Arnold, Augusta Foote, *The Sea-Beach at Ebb-Tide*. Dover Publications, 1968.

Barnes, Robert D., *Invertebrate Zoology*. W. B. Saunders, 1963.

Buchsbaum, Ralph, *Animals without Backbones: An Introduction to the Invertebrates*. The University of Chicago Press, 1948.

Buchsbaum, Ralph, and Lorus J. Milne, *The Lower Animals*. Doubleday, 1962.

*Carson, Rachel, *The Sea Around Us*. Oxford University Press, 1961.

Cromie, William J., *The Living World of the Sea*. Prentice-Hall 1966.

Curtis, Helena, *The Marvelous Animals: An Introduction to the Protozoa*. The Natural History Press, 1968.

*Darwin, Charles, *The Voyage of the Beagle*. Doubleday, 1962.

*De Kruif, Paul, *Microbe Hunters*. Harcourt Brace Jovanovich, 1966.

Dubos, René, *The Unseen World*. Rockefeller, 1962.

Grzimek, Bernard, ed., *Grzimek's Animal Life Encyclopedia*. Van Nostrand Reinhold, 1974.

Hall, Richard, *Protozoa: The Simplest of All Animals*. Holt, Rinehart & Winston, 1971.

Hardy, Alister, *The Open Sea*. Houghton Mifflin, 1965.

*Jahn, L., *How to Know Protozoa*. William C. Brown, 1949.

Kaestner, Alfred, *Invertebrate Zoology*. Vols. 1 and 3; John Wiley, 1967.

Larousse Encyclopedia of the Animal World. Larousse, 1975.

MacKinnon, Doris, and R. S. Hawes, *Introduction to the Study of Protozoa*. Oxford University Press, 1961.

*Morton, J. E., *Molluscs*. Harper & Brothers, 1960.

Parks, Peter, *Underwater Life*. Hamlyn, 1976.

Schmitt, Waldo L., *Crustaceans*. The University of Michigan Press, 1965.

Index